COST OPTIMISATION

A WAY TO CONVERT EXPENSE INTO ASSET

S.B. KUMAR

INDIA • SINGAPORE • MALAYSIA

Notion Press

Old No. 38, New No. 6
McNichols Road, Chetpet
Chennai - 600 031

First Published by Notion Press 2018
Copyright © S.B. Kumar 2018
All Rights Reserved.

ISBN 978-1-64429-258-7

This book has been published with all efforts taken to make the material error-free after the consent of the author. However, the author and the publisher do not assume and hereby disclaim any liability to any party for any loss, damage, or disruption caused by errors or omissions, whether such errors or omissions result from negligence, accident, or any other cause.

No part of this book may be used, reproduced in any manner whatsoever without written permission from the author, except in the case of brief quotations embodied in critical articles and reviews.

Dedicated To

My parents

(Late Shri R.P. Sinha & Late Smt. Ramsamhari Sinha)

Who carried me on their shoulders and encouraged

me to touch the sky.

I am who I am because of you and I know that right now

as ever you are watching over me and blessing me.

And,

My family

My wife Sanju for keeping the faith in me and

encouraging me to embark on this journey.

My lovely daughters Shivani and Shahiba for

keeping my tea warm and my heart warmer while I

burned mid night oil writing this book.

My son Shashank for the valuable IT support.

And,

To all the nuts and bolts and tools and grease that

made me the engineer I am today.

PROFIT = TOTAL REVENUE—(minus) TOTAL COSTS

Before 1990, there was producer driven market & the above formula was like below:

SALES PRICE = MANUFACTURING COST + PROFIT

Producers were producing their products by any method, at any cost and adding their desired profit in that, to fix the selling price. It means, selling prices were fixed by producers. Customers were helpless because they don't have multiple suppliers for same items.

Now, scene has changed.

Competition…competition…competition!

Competition for the best features, for the best quality, for the lowest cost, for the right time delivery & at right locations because now there are many producers for the same/similar products in the market. Producers are fighting for their survival. Now customer is the king because they offer sale price as target for producing the product.

Producers are forced to control cost otherwise they will be no more in the competition. Now threat for survival is there.

What Is Profit?

Profit means, the surplus remaining after total costs are deducted from total revenue, and the basis on which tax is computed and dividend is paid. It is the best known measure of success for any business.

What Is Total Revenue?

The total amount of money that a company actually receives during a specific period, including discounts and deductions for any return of sold products. It is the TOP LINE or GROSS INCOME figure from which costs are subtracted to determine income.

What Is Total Costs?

The total cost is the actual cost incurred in the production of a given level of output. In other words, the total costs incurred both explicit and implicit, on the resources to obtain a certain level of output, is called the Total Cost.

Total Cost = (Total fixed cost + Total Variable Cost)

What Is Total Fixed Cost?

Fixed costs do not change with output. Company/Firm must pays these even if they are shutdown. For clarification, see some examples of basic fixed costs:

- Rental costs of business building,
- The costs of leasing or purchasing of capital equipment,
- the annual business rate charged by local authorities, the costs of employing full-time contracted salaried staffs,
- the cost of meeting interest payments on loans, the depreciation of fixed capital and costs of business assurance.

Based on the above definition and examples, fixed costs are overhead costs of any business.

Average Fixed cost (AFC) = Total Fixed costs (Rupees)/Total output (Q)

What Is Variable Cost?

Variable Costs vary directly with output. When output is zero, variable costs should be zero **but as production increases, total variable costs will increase.**

For clarification, let us see some examples as follows:

- Basic raw material cost,
- Wages of workmen,
- child parts,
- tooling cost,
- electricity cost,
- consumable cost,
- energy costs,
- commission bonuses etc.

Average Variable cost (AVC) = Total variable costs (Rupees.)/Total output (Q)

We will again look at first equation to understand in-details, so that required actions can be decided without much confusion.

PROFIT = Total Revenues [minus] Total costs

- ***PROFIT is the main objective of any business.***
- PROFIT is not an optional choice; but the purpose of any business.
- PROFIT is the top most goal for any organization.
- ***PROFIT is even in dream of any businessman.***
- PROFIT is the first point of the wish list of any plant.
- PROFIT is the highly motivating factor for any organization.
- ***PROFIT is the reason for appointment of employees, procurement of machines & RM***

So, every management wants to increase the PROFIT. Many new projects wait in annual budget for declaration of profit. *It is singular goal for selection of the best machine, the best technology, the best talent, the best quality of RM, desire to introduce/implement the best manufacturing system.*

The major & silent question is:

HOW to get **PROFIT?**

HOW to improve **PROFIT?**

"**HOW?**"—is the biggest question for all.

Am I Right?

You are either owner of the plant or employees of the plant but the same question will be in your mind too & at this moment also. Sometimes we try to search some short-cut route to get PROFIT early and in huge. These wishes are natural for any progressive persons but unfortunately success does not have any short-cut route. Sometime if achieved but this will not repeat once more.

Getting profit or improving profitability has a very systematic approach, which should be followed *religiously, repeatedly, regularly by all*, to get the consistent results (Desired PROFIT).

What is that Approach?

Simple... Very simple!

Spending less and Making more!

Making more for selling more, and not keeping more in stocks.

Total revenue (sales value) depends on quantity sold and at sales price of the product.

If you will make more, you can sell more but the real owner of the sale price decision lies in hands of customers. If you keep higher sell price then there are the maximum chances that your sales quantity will be very low. Again the equation will be same, lower quantities sale at higher price resulted low revenue.

CUSTOMER is the KING!

- *A SATISFIED CUSTOMER is like god for any businessman.*
- *A SATISFIED & REPETITIVE CUSTOMER is the base for branded company!*
- *A SATISFIED, REPETITIVE & SUPPORTIVE CUSTOMER is the foundation for being GREAT COMPANY.*

So, before starting actions, we have to identify our weakness & threat for survival or growth, considering our strengths & available opportunities in the market.

Let us understand SWOT analysis in details to identify opportunities for improvements.

S.W.O.T Analysis

The SWOT analysis is a useful technique for understanding your Strengths and Weakness, and for identifying both the Opportunities open to you and the Threats, you face.

The SWOT frame work will help you to focus your activities on areas where you are strong and where the greatest opportunities lie.

It discovers new opportunities for the business & manage and eliminates Threats.

It is a strategic marketing and planning tools, for auditing an organization and it's environment.

Objective

We should aim to turn out **weakness into strengths**, and **our threats into opportunities.**

The main objective/purpose of the analysis has to be, to add value to our products and services, so that we can attract new customers, retain loyal customers, and extend products and services to customer segments over the long-term. If undertaken successfully, we can then increase our ROI (Return on Investment).

Then finally, SWOT will give managers an option to match internal strengths with external opportunities.

Outcome

The outcome should be an increase in VALUE for customers—which hopefully will improve our competitive advantages.

RULES for the BEST RESULTS

- Be realistic about the strengths and weakness of your organization.
- It should distinguish between where your organization is today, and where it could be in future.
- It should always be specific, avoid grey areas.
- Always apply the tool in relation to your competition.
- It is subjective.

Bullets are

By looking at yourself and your competitors, using the SWOT framework, you can start to craft a strategy that helps you to distinguish yourself from your competitors, so that you can compete successfully in your market.

Deep thoughts……can help you to uncover opportunities that you are well placed to exploit and by understanding the weaknesses of your business, you can manage and eliminate Threats that would otherwise catch you unawares.

Strengths

Strengths are resources and capabilities that can be used for competitive advantage.

Strength is a positive internal factor.

Consider your strengths from both – an internal perspective, and from the point of view of your customers and related people in your market.

Looking at your strengths and ask yourself whether these open up any opportunities.

How You Will Identify Your Strengths?

Try writing down a list of your Organization's characteristics based on following few questions:

- What do you do well?
- What are your unique expertise/skills?
- What advantages does your organization have?
- What do you do better than anyone else? Better than your competitors?
- What do people in your market see as your strengths?
- What are your organization's unique propositions?
- Where are you the most profitable in your business?
- Do you have exclusive access to high grade natural resources?
- Do you have exclusive patented products?

- Do you have a new, innovative products or services to offer?
- Are you carrying strong brand name?
- Location of your business compared to your competitors, is superlative?
- Carrying good reputations in society/market/among vendors/employees?
- Can supply superlative quality at lower price?
- Having excellent working conditions?
- Your manufacturing system is at par with your competitors or World class level?
- Able to respond quickly/the shortest lead time for products developments?
- Internal products/Dies/Tools design capability better than competitors?
- Low over heads, so you can offer good value to customers?
- Having state of the art R&D centre for your products?
- Having simulation techniques to assure reliability of products life?
- Flat organizations for quick decision making?
- Can provide wide range of products?
- Speed & reliability of delivery is superlative as compared to competitors?
- LEAN Manufacturing/TPM/Kaizen Culture/TQM/Continual improvements are in place?
- Highly experienced product related team availability?
- Favourable access of distribution network?

Weaknesses

Weakness is a negative internal factor.

Look at your weaknesses and ask yourself whether you could open up opportunities by eliminating them.

It's best to be realistic now, and face any unpleasant truth as soon as possible.

HOW will you identify your weaknesses?

By brainstorming/data based on following few questions:

- What parts of your business are not profitable?
- In what areas do you need to improve?
- What do you do badly?
- What should you avoid?
- What are people in your market likely to see as weakness?
- What factors lose your sales/customers?
- Do you have ineffective and high cost structure?
- Are your competitors doing anything better than you?
- They have better mfg system than you?
- What resources do you lack?
- Weak brand name?
- Weakness in catalogue & website?
- Working culture is not at par with your competitors?
- Carrying poor reputation among vendors/customers/employees/society?
- Lack of required funding for updating of new technology?
- Weak internal communication system?
- Lack of marketing expertise?
- Location of your business is not attractive?
- Cost & Quality are not attractive to your customers?
- QMS is not truthfully implemented on floor?
- Customer complaints handling team is not strong & trained?

Honesty in this will help you a lot!

Opportunities

An opportunity is a positive external factor.

Think deeply, what are the business goals you are currently working towards? How can you do more with your existing customers or clients?

Convert your Threats to opportunity.

How will you find the real potential opportunities?

By brainstorming/data based supported with your past experience in the same field and get clue from following questions:

- ✓ How can you turn your strength into opportunities?
- ✓ What opportunities are open to you?
- ✓ Our business sector is expanding with many future opportunities for success?
- ✓ Our competitors are slow to adopt new technologies?
- ✓ Local government wants to encourage local business?
- ✓ How can you use technology to enhance your business?
- ✓ What interesting trends are you aware of?
- ✓ Are there new target audiences you have to potential to reach?
- ✓ Changes in technology and markets on both a broad and narrow scale?
- ✓ Changes in government policy related to your field?
- ✓ Arrival of new technology?
- ✓ A developing market such as internet?
- ✓ Mergers, joint ventures or strategic alliances?
- ✓ Moving into new market segments that offer improved profits?
- ✓ A new international market?
- ✓ Certified QMS/Manufacturing system better than your competitors?
- ✓ A market vacated by ineffective competitors?
- ✓ Huge potential in unfulfilled customer needs?

Threats

A Threat is negative external factor.

If you can act for elimination, then it could be value addition.

"PEST ANALYSIS" can help to ensure that you don't overlook external factors such as government regulations or technology changes in your industries.

Pest Analysis

Scanning the business environment.

It is used for identifying "BIG PICTURE" opportunities and Threats.

- P = Political changes
- E = Economic changes
- S = Socio-cultural changes
- T = Technological changes in your business environment.

This help you to understand the "Big Picture" forces of change that you are exposed to, and from this, take advantage of the opportunities that they present.

Benefits

- It helps you to spot business or personal opportunities, and it gives you advanced warning of significant threats.
- It reveals the direction of change within your business environment. This helps you to shape what you are doing, so that you work with change rather than again.

How Will You Identify Threats?

Again by brainstorming/data based. By generating clues from following few questions:

- What obstacle do you face?
- What is the strength of your biggest competitors?

- What are your competitors doing that you are not?
- A new competitor in your home market?
- Price war with competitors?
- Your competitors have a new, innovative products or services?
- No readymade market for your products?
- Your Manufacturing system is much inferior than competitors?
- Your customer care or customer complaints team is weaker compared to competitors?
- Is changing technology threatening your position?
- Do you have cash flow problem?
- Currently changed market trends?
- New regulations?
- New substitute products?
- Could any of your weakness seriously threaten your business?
- Competitors have superior access to channel of distributions?

Swot Tips

- Only accept precise, verifiable statements for analysis & actions.
- Ruthlessly prune long lists of factors and prioritise them, so that you spend your time thinking about the most significant factors.
- Make sure that options generated are carried through to later stages in the strategy formation process.
- Apply it at the right level (Product or process line levels).
- Use it in conjunction with: USP Analysis, Core competence Analysis & PEST analysis.

USP Analysis

The unique selling proposition (USP): Finding your competitive edge.

Your USP is the unique thing that you can offer that your competitors can't. It is your competitive edge. It is the reason why your customers buy from you and you alone.

- ✓ Understand the characteristics that customer's value. Do the brainstorming with knowledgeable people in the process like sales persons, customer service team, Manufacturing head, Quality head and customers themselves.
- ✓ Rank yourself and your competitors by these criteria. Identify your top competitors. Score yourself and each of your competitors out of 10 for each characteristic. It should be based on objective data or try to make your best guess.
- ✓ Identify where you rank well. Plot these points on graph.
- ✓ Preserve your USP and use it.
- ✓ Finally you look at how you will defend and build your USP as competition evolves.

Core Competencies Analysis

Objective: To get ahead of your competition and stay ahead.

By using this idea, you will make the very most of the opportunities open to you.

- ✓ You will focus on your efforts so that you develop an unique level of expertise in areas that matter to your customers. Because of this, you will command the reward that comes with this expertise.
- ✓ You will learn to develop your own skills in a wat that complements your company's core competencies.

How to Use It?

- ✓ Brainstorm the factors that are important to your clients.
- ✓ Brainstorm your existing competencies and the things you do well.
- ✓ For the list of your own competencies, screen them against the tests of relevance, difficulty of imitation and breadth of

application; see any of the competencies you have listed are core competencies.
- ✓ For the list of factors that are important to clients, screen them using these tests to see if you could develop these as core competencies.
- ✓ Review the two screened lists and think about them:
    a) If you have identified core competencies that you already have, then great. Work on them and make sure that you build them as far as sensibly possible.
    b) If you have no core competencies then look at ones that you could develop and work to build them.
- ✓ Think of the most time consuming and costly things that you do as a company. If any of these things do not contribute to a core competence, ask yourself if you can outsource them effectively, clearing down time so that you can focus on core competencies.

Finally, Be Harsh!

- You have probably written down lots and lots of ideas, but now is the time to cut prune and organise what you have come up with.
- Prioritise specific and fully costed ideas, so you can work with the most usable first.
- Put the more general suggestions to one side, ready to be discussed and expanded later.

Action Plan

One of the most important parts of your SWOT Analysis is using the data you compiled to identify new strategies and goals for your business.

- Create a plan to build up your strength even more.
- List ways you can work on building up your weakness.

- Set SMART goals for each of the opportunities you identified.
- Devise a plan to use your strengths to decrease the threats you identified.
  Then look for ways to combine data from different quadrants in even more ways.
- Explore how you can combine your strengths and opportunities to develop new strategies.
- Try combining strengths and threats to identify threats you can eliminate.
- Look at your weakness and opportunities to create a list of areas ready for improvement.
- Make a list of areas to avoid, that fall under weakness and threats.

Once you understand how to compile your SWOT data and find ways to use it strategically, the SWOT analysis will be a tool that you can use over and over in your business to explore new opportunities and improve your decision making process.

We, all, want to make a great company, we all want to become great employer, we all want to become a great employee, we all want to become a great father, we all want to become a great lover/beloved, we all want to become a great friend for others but as you have seen above, BEING GREAT requires satisfaction, repetitive and supportive.

So, finally, if we want good PROFIT then there are only two options:

SPENDING LESS: REDUCE TOTAL COST!

MAKING MORE: INCREASE SALES!!

YES, produce **MORE** & produce **GOOD QUALITY** at **REDUCED COST!!**

Kindly see the below table as an example, I am sure that it will give you much clarity to reach at the concluding point.

Table 1

Category	Current State	Spend 10% Less	Make 10% More	Do Both
Sales	100	100	110	110
Direct Material	25	25	27,5	24.75
Direct labor	25	22.5	27.5	24.75
Fixed cost	20	20	20	20
Selling cost	15	15	16.5	14.85
Administrative cost	5	5	5	5
PROFIT	10	13.5	13.5	20.65
PROFIT increase%	—	35	35	106.5

The above example shows the positive impact of SPENDING LESS & MAKING MORE!

Case 1:

We sold same quantity and got same sales value.

We attacked on COST and got 10% cost reduction in labor cost.

In TPM language, we achieved 10% improvement in OEE.

Keeping RM consumption, Fixed cost, selling cost and administrative cost maintained as earlier.

We found fantastic results, 35% profitability improvement!

Case 2:

We improved sales by 10%. For improving sale, we have to make 10% more and resulted 10% increase in RM consumption cost, making charges as labor cost increased by 10% and selling cost also impacted by 10% (to sell more products).

Still good result, not bad! Got 35% profitability improvement from current situation.

Case 3:

We have attacked from both ends, made 10% more and reduced total cost by 10%.

Yes, miracle happened!

106.5% profitability improved...... Fantastic!

Well done team!

How to Reduce Total Costs?

Every business required some basic costs to start with, some recurring costs to maintain the business level and some costs required for breakthrough improvement. Basic costs to be maintained as per business needs but recurring costs required proper standardization and controls. Recurring costs means every minute, day, week, months and months after months.

Examples of such recurring costs are:
- Marketing Research
- Product design cost
- Raw material
- Purchasing
- storage
- Transportation
- Receipt inspection
- Product identification
- Labor cost
- consumables cost

- Energy cost
- Packing & packaging costs
- Advertisement cost
- customer complaints handling cost
- Testing
- validation
- Analysis
- Over heads
- outsourcing
- sales promotion
- communication, etc.

Broader strategies would be:

- Elimination of wastes
- Increasing productivity
- Improving processes/Operations
- Use low weight & low rate material
- Excellent input quality
- Stable, predictable and capable processes
- Improved Quality system standards

Business pattern can be broadly classified in three categories:

- Manufacturing & sales business
- Distributions & Retailing
- Any kind of services

Manufacturing business generally required bigger space, more manpower, maximum energy and consumables along with bulk raw materials & machines purchase. Whereas other two types of businesses required smaller space, fewer manpower, limited energy consumptions.

So, based upon nature of business, cost optimization focus shall be different for manufacturing and servicing sectors. Potential of savings shall be less in retailing & servicing business but even that small savings will have greater impact on profitability.

We will discuss here the different methodology of cost optimization for smaller to bigger business group (means retailing/servicing sector to manufacturing sector).

There are different types of tools and techniques being used for it like,

- ✓ Variance Analysis
- ✓ Value Analysis
- ✓ Ratio Analysis
- ✓ Just in time approach
- ✓ Standardized costing
- ✓ Total Quality control
- ✓ Economic order Quantity
- ✓ Market research
- ✓ Inventory management and control
- ✓ Benchmarking
- ✓ Budget & Budgetary control
- ✓ Work study
- ✓ Material handling
- ✓ Low cost automation
- ✓ Variety reduction
- ✓ Production control
- ✓ Material control
- ✓ Design
- ✓ Production line layout
- ✓ Breakeven analysis
- ✓ Cost per direct labor
- ✓ Separate analysis of manufacturing cost
- ✓ Impact of parts storage on labor cost
- ✓ Network analysis
- ✓ PERT/CPM applications
- ✓ Cost reduction ratio

Excess of anything gives bitter taste and results, so optimization is the best solution for better, consistent and motivated results.

Cost Can Be Reduced Through

Reduction

- ✓ **Production time**
    - ➢ Cycle time
    - ➢ Throughput time

Waiting time

- ➢ Waiting for material
- ➢ Waiting for man
- ➢ Waiting for machine
- ➢ Waiting for dies/tool setup
- ➢ Waiting for first piece inspection
- ➢ Waiting for decision

Searching time

- ➢ Searching for tools
- ➢ Searching for materials
- ➢ Searching for instruments
- ➢ Searching for hand gloves, goggles
- ➢ Searching for supervisor

Inventory

- ➢ Red inventory
- ➢ Grey inventory
- ➢ Disputed
- ➢ Slow moving
- ➢ obsolete

Raw material

- ➢ Weight (consumption}
- ➢ Rate (comparison)

- Yield per ton/kg
- Damaged during handling
- Deteriorated due to poor storage
- Shelf life

Elimination

✓ **8 wastes**

- Over production
- Over processing
- Transportation
- Waiting
- Motion losses
- Defects
- Excessive/unwanted inventory
- Low or no utilization of available resources

Bottlenecks

- Product
- Process
- Systems
- Suppliers
- Market conditions
- Customer's expectation
- Appropriate RM availability
- Appropriate machines/tools
- Appropriate technology

Barriers

- Local
- State
- central

Modification

Product

- Features
- Shape
- Size
- Models

Process

- Method of manufacturing
- Method of validation
- Method of testing
- Method of heat treatment
- Method of surface treatment
- Method of packing/packaging

Systems

- Manufacturing system
- Quality system
- Maintenance system
- Procurement system
- Advertisement system

Design

- New innovative features in same
- New product
- As per customer's expectations
- Robust
- Easy to make and control
- Low complaints & nil warranty
- No need for replacement
- Multiple features
- Better than available

Layout

- Product driven layout
- Single piece flow
- U-Shaped
- Flow manufacturing concept
- Single location
- Ergonomics
- Easy material picking & handling
- Easy for cleaning, lubrication, tightening, inspection & adjustment
- Easy to re-filling
- Easy to observe

Innovation

Breakthrough innovations, much better than your competitors, unique features, multiple features like smart phones.

- ✓ Re-engineering
- ✓ Method of producing
- ✓ Equipment
- ✓ Tooling

Cost Optimization

Cost optimization is a continual process of refinement and improvement of a system over its entire life cycle. From the initial design of your very first proof of concept to the ongoing operation of production workloads. You can adopt the practices in this book to build and operate cost aware systems that achieve business outcomes while minimizing costs, allowing your business to maximize its return on investment.

A cost optimized system will fully utilize all resources, achieve an outcome at the lowest possible price point, and meet your functional requirements. It helps in depth guidance for designing your work load and selecting your services.

Cost optimization ensures that your costs move in line with demand. It also helps in analyzing and attributing costs along with clear guidance to use appropriate resources types to minimize costs and supporting in continual reduction of costs over time.

Cost Control: The process of monitoring and regulating the expenditure of funds is known as cost control whereas the process of identifying and eliminating unnecessary costs to improve the profitability of a business is known as cost reduction.

Features of Cost Control

Cost control process involves,

- ✓ Setting targets and standards
- ✓ Ascertaining the actual performance
- ✓ Comparing the actual performance with standards
- ✓ Investigating the variances
- ✓ Taking corrective actions
- ✓ Creation of SOPs for future

The burning question is, how will you set the target and standards?

There are several methodologies which are being adopted by different business houses. Some firms directly benchmark the cost pattern from their nature of companies/service houses in their locality/state/country, some company uses their past best data as a reference for future target setting.

In my views, the later method is the most reliable and achievable. Setting the extreme target is the easiest act but the probability of success in that is the least, resulted highly demotivation among team members. Repetition of such failures gives permanent setback to firms and their leaders.

Always set **SMART** target. Such target is simple to understand, measurable, achievable, and reliable and having time bound limitations. For establishing a winning habit in the team, **SMART** target setting is the best option.

Once target is set, then the real action for performance measurement starts. The key point in performance measurement data is "authenticity of data." False data will give you false interpretation resulted useless actions and results. Now mostly manufacturing company uses high accuracy & reliable software to monitor this performance but still there are chances of wrong entry if software system does not have closed loop system.

System Poka – yoke is necessary for such type of software designing.

After these two important steps, gap (Variance) analysis becomes very easy and such consistent gap monitoring data can be used for real root cause identification for permanent actions.

Variance Analysis is defined as the difference between the expected amount and the actual amount of costs incurred. Variance analysis is the investigation of the difference between actual and planned behavior. Let us see one very simple example, If your budgeted sales target is 20000/, Actual sales performance is 16000 for any one product then variance would be 20000 -[minus] 16000 = 4000/ for that product for that period. Now we found the variance amount for this product but this much exercise for data collection will not be fruitful if we are unable to identify the reasons of variance. In many cases, variances are well known to our sales persons. But if, in reality, variance reason is not known then we should deploy scientific and systematic tools & techniques for potential/ probable and root cause identification. The most commonly used tools and techniques are: Why-why analysis, Fault tree analysis, Fish bone diagram, Brainstorming, Cause and effect diagram. After identification of real root cause, we can take corrective and preventive actions for elimination of repetition of such gaps in future months target.

Some probable causes of variance:

- Changes in productivity can alter the cost levels.
- Change in product design.
- Investment in new capital and replacement of old equipment can have impact on: operating cost & overhead costs.
- Changes in days and working hours

Value Analysis (VA)

Value = Worth to you/Price paid by you

Value is the minimum money that has to be expended in purchasing or manufacturing a product to create the appropriate use or esteem factor.

In a nut shell, Value is the ratio between a function for customer satisfaction and the cost of that function.

Function: The effect produced by a product or by one of its elements, in order to satisfy customer needs.

Value Analysis is a methodology to increase the value of an object to be analyzed could be an existing or a new product or process, and it is usually accomplished by a team following a work plan. In other words, it is a process of systematic review that is applied to existing product designs in order to compare the function of the product required by a customer to meet their requirements at the lowest cost consistent with the specified performance and reliability needed.

Value can be broadly categorized in 4 parts:

- ➢ Utility Value: It is called as functional value also. How useful/functional the product is seen to be.
- ➢ Esteem Value: The value that customer/user gives to product attributes (properties, features, or attractiveness), not directly contributing to utility but more relating to aesthetic and subjective value.

- ➤ Cost Value: The sum of labor, material and various other costs required for producing a product.
- ➤ Exchange Value: its properties or qualities which enable us to exchange it for something else, we want.

> Value of product = Performance of the function/costs
> Best Value = Low cost + Justified additions

Application of Value Analysis

- Capital goods: Plant, Equipment, machinery, tools.
- Raw material and semi-processed material, including fuel.
- Material handling and transportation costs.
- Purchased parts, components sub-assemblies etc.
- Maintenance, repairs, and operational items.
- Finishing items such as paints, oils and varnishes etc.
- Packing and packaging materials.
- Printing and stationery items.
- Miscellaneous items of regular consumptions.
- Power, water supply, air, steam and other utilities.

Value analysis is an effective tool for cost reduction and the results accomplished are far greater.

- It improves the effectiveness of work.
- It is an organized approach to a problem.
- It is value, applied at the design stage itself.
- It reduces unnecessary costs, obvious and hidden which can be eliminated without adversely affecting quality, efficiency and safety.

Objectives of Value Analysis

- To provide better value to a product/service.
- To improve the company's competitive position.

- To ensure that every element of cost – labor, materials, suppliers & service contribute equally to the function of the product.
- To eliminate unnecessary cost.

Steps to Be Followed

- Establish the objectives (Cost reduction).
- Analyze the production process of the supplier company.
- Decompose various characteristics of purchased product.
- Hold a creative brainstorming session to explore all alternative possibilities.
- Sort the ideas to establish the cost of each function.
- Select the best alternative.
- Develop a plan for implementing the change.

Techniques of Value Analysis

- ✓ Design analysis
- ✓ Check lists preparation
- ✓ Brainstorming
- ✓ Price analysis

7 steps implementation procedures:

- ➢ Selection and orientation
- ➢ Analysis
- ➢ Recording ideas
- ➢ Innovation/creativity
- ➢ Evaluation
- ➢ Recommendation
- ➢ Implementation & monitoring

Descriptions of Each Step

- **Selection & orientation:** To select those critical areas where a potential for cost reductions is expected.

Use the common Pareto chart or ABC analysis.
General scope, restrictions and aim of the study is defined.

- **Analysis:** Examine the data at a VA group team meeting.

    Kindly record, minutes of each brainstorming sessions.
    Apply the tests for value.
    Propose further actions.

- **Recording ideas:** write down the minutes of analyses meetings and circulate it.

    It includes agenda for next meetings too.

- **Innovation/creativity:** Arrange team meetings in order to discuss the ideas analyzed and any new information obtained.

    Think upon practical measures for reducing costs and increasing value.

- **Evaluation:** investigate suggestions for reducing costs and to make them practical and acceptable to client management.

    Obtain definite prices and costs in order to estimate cost reductions accurately.

- **Recommendation:** recommend cost reduction to client management.

    Present the recommendations in a comprehensive report.
    Recommend a member to act as an implementation consultant for VA recommendations.

- **Implementation & monitoring:** implement the recommendations accepted by the company management. Monitor the results as suggested in VA report.

    Note down the feedback of the management upon completion of VA assignments.

Benefits of Value Analysis

- Better purchasing techniques.
- Better suppliers and manufacturing methods.
- Lower operating costs.
- Standardization and re-evaluation.
- Substitution & packaging.
- Better material handling.
- Better inventory control.
- Lower maintenance and overhead costs.

What Is "VALUE STREAM?"

Before going into details, we must be aware about some needed disciplines:

- Lean system implementation requires a high degree of discipline and sometimes it can stress the workforce.
- There is high level of co-operation & trust required between operators and supervisors.
- Reward systems and labor classifications must often be revamped when a lean system is implemented.
- Existing layouts may need to be changed.
- Daily production schedules in high-volume, make-to-stock environments must be stable for extended periods.
- If the inventory advantages of a lean system are to be realized. Small lot sizes must be used.
- If frequent, small shipments of purchased items cannot be arranged with suppliers, large inventory savings for these items cannot be realized.

Here, we will discuss in brief, what is actually Lean process?

Define value from the customer's perspective—Map the Value stream—Create Flow; eliminate the root causes of waste—Create pull where flow is difficult to achieve—seek perfection via continuous improvement—!!!!

VSM—Why?—What?—& where?

- It is a key tool for Lean implementation, makes process and problems visible.
- Forms the basis of an improvement plan and a common language.
- Highlights suppliers, inputs, process, outputs and customers (SIPOC).
- It is a qualitative tool for identifying and eliminating waste (or Muda).
- It aligns organizations processes, creates a sense of teamwork/ownership.
- It involves drawing—current state, future state, & an implementation plan.
- In spans of the entire value chain from raw materials receipts to finished goods delivery.
- A paper and pencil tool to help you visualize and understand the linkage between material and information flow.
- It focuses on maximizing the overall flow.

Value Added and Non-Value Added Activities

Value added = any activity, for which, the customer is willing to pay, others are waste.

- Who are your customers?
- What do they really want?

To be considered "Value added," a process step must have YES to all these questions.

- Does the customer care for this effort?
- Does it change the thing?
- Is it done right the first time?
- Is it required by law or regulation?

Non-Value added= any activity that consumes time and/or resources & does not add value to the service or product for the customer. These activities should be *eliminated, simplified, reduced, or integrated.*

- Necessary—legal/regulatory requirements
- Unnecessary—waiting, unnecessary processing, defects, motion (people), Transportation (product), underutilized people, inventory.

Principles of Value Stream Mapping

- ➢ Diagnostic tool:
    - It reveals hidden symptoms of larger problems.
- ➢ Strategic planning Activity:
    - Helps to prioritize opportunities for improvement.
    - Results in an implementation plan.
- ➢ Macro-level-Visual representation
    - Information flow
    - People and material flow
    - Each process block represents a handoff or a break in the time line.
- ➢ Contains relevant metrics
    - Lead time—Throughput/turnaround/flow time
    - Cycle time—Touch/process time

Some Key Definitions

Cycle Time (C/T)—Time to complete a single unit of production.

First Time Through (FTT)—% of jobs that are complete and accurate the first time that they are processed.

Demand—Average number of units per shift.

Batch Size (BS)—size of typical batch that is processed as a unit.

TAKT time—Rate of demand.

Throughput time—Sum of delays and process time.

Process Ratio—Total process time/Throughput time.

Value added Ratio—Total value added time/Throughput time.

Current Process Challenges

- Lots of waiting.
- Lots of travel.
- Lack of communication.
- Lack of skills/not trained.
- Too many handoffs.
- Too many approvals
- Too many workarounds
- Duplicate of work
- Dead zones—places where work gets held up or lost.
- Lost time—people looking for work and/or re-work loops to correct errors.
- Broken interfaces—ineffective or non-existent interfaces
- Different prioritization rules in different departments.
- High lead time (slow throughput/turnaround).
- High WIP (Waste in process—bottleneck/backlogs)
- Low CT/LT ratio (Lots of waiting)

These Are Few Examples of Costs, Generally Incurred in Manufacturing Industries

1. *Use of excessive Raw material.*
2. *Higher rate of purchase of RM.*
3. *Poor/unbalanced procurement planning.*
4. *High rework% age with existing process.*
5. *High rejection% age with existing process.*

6. *Rejection/rework more due to skipping from approved SOP.*
7. *Lack of process audit by experienced engineer/manager.*
8. *Expenses in customer complaints handling.*
9. *Multiple materials handling within plant.*
10. *Double/multiple touching of materials for the same operations.*
11. *Selection of poor capability of suppliers (considered only lower cost, not quality).*
12. *Deployment of excessive manpower.*
13. *Appointment & retention of negative attitude manpower.*
14. *Continuation with low efficiency manpower.*
15. *Continuation with physically unfit manpower.*
16. *Low experience & unskilled manpower.*
17. *Absenteeism more than 3% of the plant.*
18. *Presence of various types of leakages:*

    - *Water,*
    - *Coolant,*
    - *Oil,*
    - *Air,*
    - *Secret information.*

19. *Low productivity compared to rated machine capacity.*
20. *Huge unwanted production (Production not as per customer demands/Push system production/over production).*
21. *Unplanned & Unexpected machine breakdown resulted whole line stoppage.*
22. *Initial start-up losses (Beginning of the shift).*
23. *Minor stoppages during processes.*
24. *Material/tool/documents searching time more.*
25. *More waiting time for correct man/machine/material.*
26. *Zig-zag layout.*
27. *Insufficient & wrong communications.*
28. *Late communications.*
29. *Living with old technology (High cost, low output).*
30. *Unbalanced cycle time.*

31. *Cycle time more than TAKT time.*
32. *Delay decisions.*
33. *Delay selections.*
34. *Higher developments lead time.*
35. *Agenda less review meetings/many meetings/without preparation meeting/without information meeting/without concrete decision meeting.*
36. *Multiple mails as reminder on same subjects.*
37. *Regularly late coming in factory of important employees.*
38. *Late sitting in office due to low efficiency/improper work planning.*
39. *High energy efficient & low output machine/Use of generalised machine.*
40. *Irrelevant data collection/sharing & analysis.*
41. *Low or no customer demands of profitable items.*
42. *Delay despatches to customer.*
43. *Poor packing & Packaging of materials (Not as per customer expectations).*
44. *Wrong labelling & wrong mode of material despatches.*
45. *Old designed products (Without proper implementation of ECNs).*
46. *Partial delivery of most customers' wanted materials.*
47. *Damages during transportation due to negligence of drivers.*
48. *Delivery of unwanted materials to customers.*
49. *Skipping of preventive maintenance.*
50. *Non-maintenance of required needed spare parts stocks of critical machines.*
51. *Poor storage area (full of dusts, overheat, more moisture).*
52. *High set up time.*
53. *Bigger batch sizes of production.*
54. *Low yield.*
55. *Long walking distance due to poor layout.*
56. *Manual material handling.*
57. *Higher repair & maintenance cost.*
58. *Frequent repair & maintenance needed due to misalignments.*
59. *Huge grey & red inventory.*

60. *Higher green inventory.*
61. *Material kept more than 5 feet height.*
62. *Material kept in rack and pallets (slow movement/extra efforts for picking & handling).*
63. *Wrong process sequence.*
64. *Procedure for 100% visual inspection by same person on daily basis.*
65. *Short cut in operation cycle time.*
66. *High & low temperature in heat treatment operation.*
67. *High & low pressure in mfg & testing of products.*
68. *Poor lighting in shop floor especially near inspection point.*
69. *Noisy working environment.*
70. *Poor tool design & management.*
71. *Dirty & dangerous heat treatment shop.*
72. *Procurement of robots/fully automatic machine without line balancing.*
73. *No low cost automation in the plant for monotonous job.*
74. *Low VAPCO (Value added per person contributions) due to negative attitude.*
75. *Low inventory turnover ratio.*
76. *Unhealthy working environment (dark, dry, hot, humid, slippery, smoky).*
77. *Untrained casual workmen at critical operation.*
78. *Taking out multi pages coloured prints for internal uses.*
79. *Unsafe actions in the plant.*
80. *Unsafe conditions in the plant.*
81. *Disposal of unwanted materials at low price (No policy for 3 quotations).*
82. *Over writing/no highlighting of critical information.*
83. *Delay disposal of unwanted materials.*
84. *No disposal of unwanted machines/materials.*
85. *Unavailability of SOPs.*
86. *Idle running of machines.*
87. *Low process capability of machines.*
88. *Multiple inspections/over quality.*

89. *Low life of machine spare parts (Genuine spares).*
90. *High variations in repeatability & reproducibility (R&R).*
91. *Frequent power failure & no back up of CNC machines.*
92. *Culture of low talent retention.*
93. *Lack of regular & proper cleaning of machines (not only outer body of machine).*
94. *Lack of lubrication of rotating & sliding parts.*
95. *Manual checking of variable parameters with mechanical instruments for accuracy.*
96. *Use of low grade lubricating oils (not as per specified grades).*
97. *Premature failure of products at customer end/field.*
98. *Dissatisfied customers.*
99. *Dissatisfied employees.*
100. *Dissatisfied suppliers.*
101. *High consumable consumptions.*

But, from Where to Start?

People first,

> *Positive people are assets,*

> *So, team formation first!*

Then,

Identification, prioritization, Actions, reviews/assessment, course corrections, presentation, celebration & finally next bottleneck identification!!

Ratio Analysis

A ratio analysis is defined as an arithmetical/quantitative/numerical relationship between two performance parameters. It is actually used for comparison. Comparative graph is plotted between readings of one company with another for setting the benchmarking standard.

So, it is mainly used as external standards, that is, for comparing performance with the other organization in the industry. We can also use this ratio analysis to validate our internal performance. It is a statistical yardstick that provides a measure of the relationship between two figures for the same business.

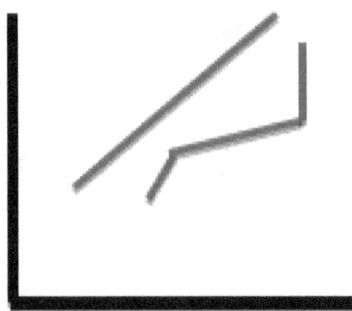

It may be expressed in percentage terms or absolute numbers as a proportion.

For better understanding and required controls of any plant, we can use different types of performance monitoring sets as to identify department wise some key performance indicators. Few examples are mentioned below:

PRODUCE MORE and SPEND LESS

Production increases, Breakdown decreases! Breakdown and total loss hours are costs. B/D and total loss hours to be eliminated by TPM implementation!

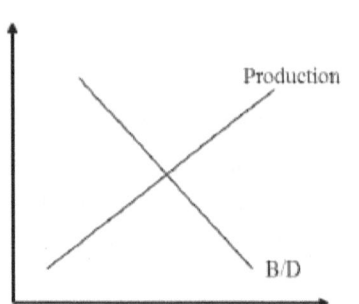
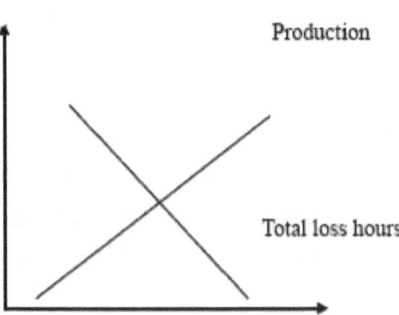

Production increases but manufacturing cost should be increased. We have seen much such presentation where plant manager only present production increase trend in one slide and expect clapping but truthfully manufacturing cost increased more than proportion. This should not be appreciated by review committee.

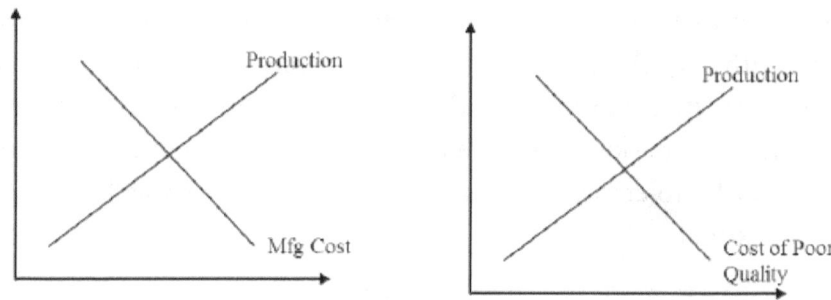

The similar situation exists when we show only production increase graphs during review and always silent for cost of poor quality. Cost of poor quality is one type of national loss if we don't learn from previous mistake and reasons for rejections are repetitive in nature. Actually we transform a good quality of raw material in poor quality of final products. Reduction & elimination of such costs directly add value in balance sheet and plant becomes profitable. 80–90% quality defects are due to negligence and by following short cut especially in night shift.

Generally, we see in actual situation that when production increases, energy cost also increases beyond proportion. Such situation happens due to extra hours working to meet the targeted quantity,

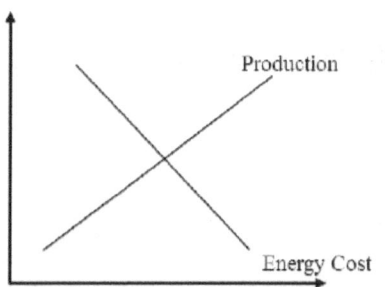
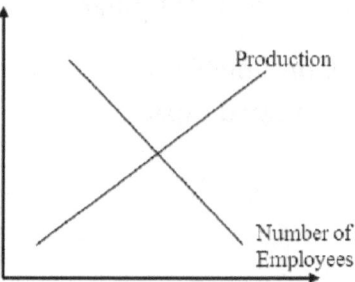

Production increases are good but to achieve higher quantity, the deployment of more manpower is not good. Efficiency improvement means, more output with same or reduced manpower. Reducing manpower for cost reduction is not highly appreciable but increasing manpower due to cover low efficiency is the worst. We must identify the real root cause of low efficiency. It could be due to monotonous job, it could be low understanding of right methods or it could be due to poor health also. All these causes can be eliminated by providing good & timely assistance to those workmen but some cases we have seen that few workmen are slow in nature or by intentions. Those bad intentions should not be tolerated by plant at all. Such workmen will spoil many good workmen.

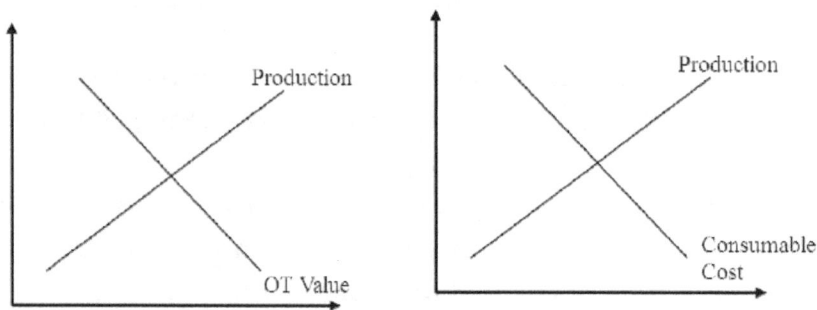

OT is a common word in manufacturing sector. OT = Over time, is an additional cost if deployed for coverage of low efficiency in such cases also when machines are not capable to meet the targeted quantity either due to small stoppages or may be old technology. Minor stoppages can be eliminated by implementation of JISHU HOZEN (7 steps) of TPM pillar.

Consumable cost increase is basically due to leakages or working at beyond rated capacity.

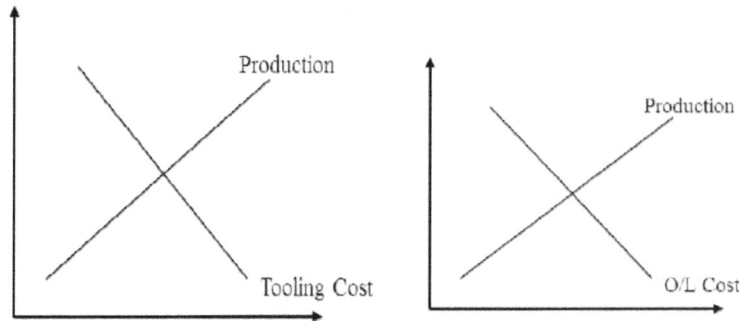

The above trend is the burning examples for even many SMEs that they should not only monitor production increase only but if we are focusing on cost optimization then we must monitor for tool life too. If production increases and tool consumption costs also increases then it will be useless data monitoring. If tool consumption cost decreases with production increase then it will be appreciable act. Finally we can fix per piece tool cost for benchmarking and that reference will be future base for improvement.

O/L = offloading cost (outsourcing cost). Many companies now choose to outsource some time consuming and low value addition work to outside, some has internal capacity constraints and some has unavailability of such machine in house. In such cases, our main objective would be outsourcing cost reduction with increase of production. If required, we should help and upgrade our suppliers by helping them for implementation of 5S, Kaizen, SMED, Lean manufacturing and quality improvement tools & techniques,

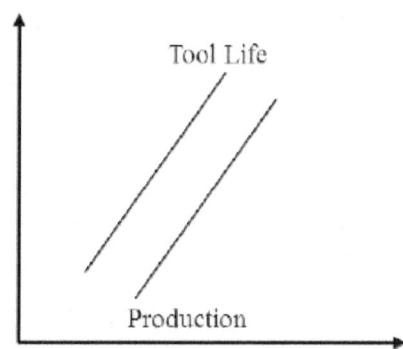

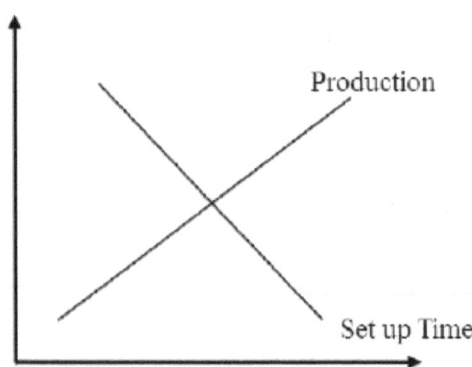

The above relationship diagram shows that when set up time reduces then production must be increased. Mostly world class manufacturing company is trying to achieve set up time in single digit. SMED = single minute exchange of dies. The detail case study done at one of the biggest plant (In the field of rigid plastic container manufacturing company), you can read in my book (PRE-FIT for PROFIT).

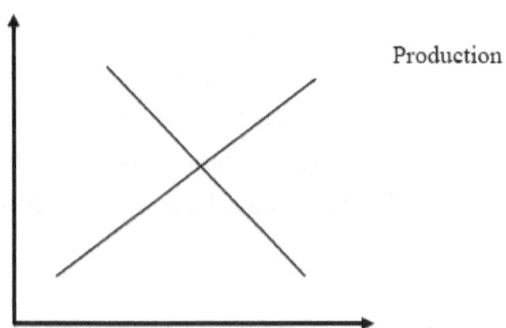

Material Cost

It is the most important relationship graph. It is universal truth that when production will increase then material cost is bound to increase but ratio/standards to be maintained, We have seen in many cases that when production quantities increased then shop manager forgot to track the material consumption ratio resulted high consumption of material, material wasted in high rejections, material purchased at very higher cost to meet the customer demand, material transported through air lifting too.

When such situation will happen then higher production is certainly not a boon. It will not help in balance sheet at all. Material traveling distance

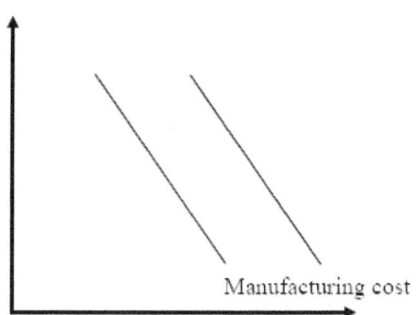

If material traveling distance reduced by re-layout of production line, then overall manufacturing cost must be reduced, especially when material handling is being done manually. Those deployed manpower to be removed from there and arrange for his/their training and finally deploy them on some value addition work.

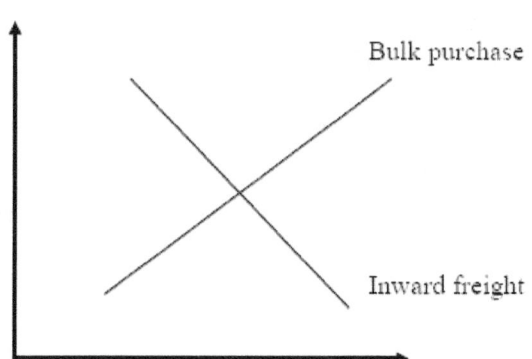

If inward freights are reducing when sales are increasing or when we are doing bulk purchase then these actions and data are highly supportive for profit maximization. Freight cost is not a smaller segment in overall purchasing costs.

Some company uses their dedicated trucks/vehicles, some associated with trade union. Few companies opted for "MILK RUN" concept. (MILK RUN = vehicle goes to multiple suppliers and collects different parties materials for the same city and accordingly unloaded all consignments to right customers.

What's objective of any plant when they plan to attend trade fair and exhibition? You will find only one answer – to attract new customer, to get new business and to increase the sales. If this happened as expected then it will be value addition move otherwise it will again increase your cost. Only participating in exhibition/trade fair is not enough but presenting

Companies as per customer's needs are the key points. Many organizations just commit very tall talk by discussing their visionary plan but they generally fail during follow up audit and that half opened door closed permanently.

So participating in such types of mega show is good but not without real commitment for improvement.

P-Q analysis Vs Procurement cost: Here "P" stands for production & Q stands for quantity. In this, we prepare one list from the highest production quantities to the lowest for making strategic decisions for production preparation without missing a single quantity of customer demands.

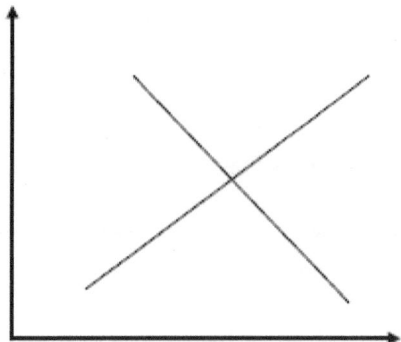

Real P-Q analysis is the cumulative average production of last 12 months. This list gives the nearly correct statistics of actual productions which finally helps in procurement planning. You can plan bulk quantities with proper comparison and competitions between 2–3 good suppliers. By doing this, procurement cost can be reduced.

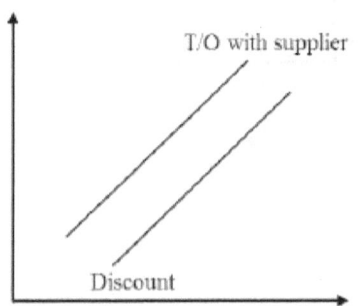

46 | Cost Optimisation

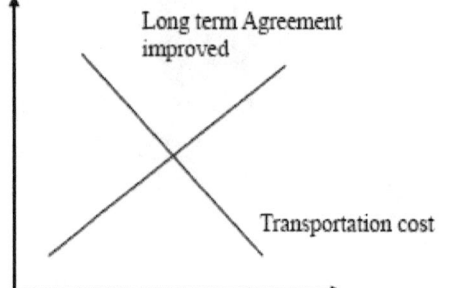

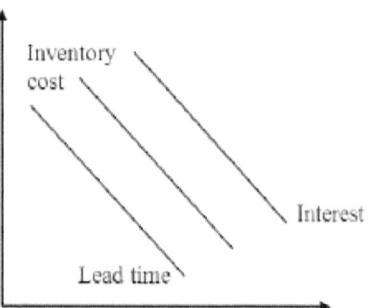

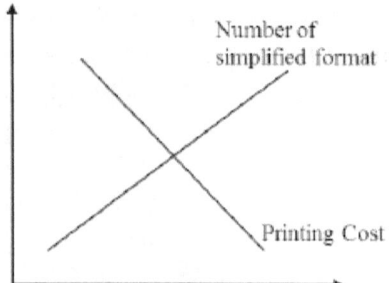

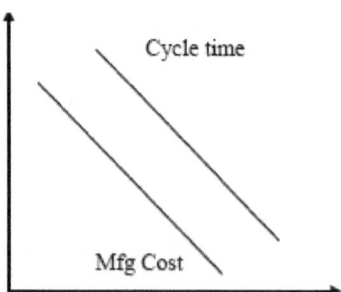

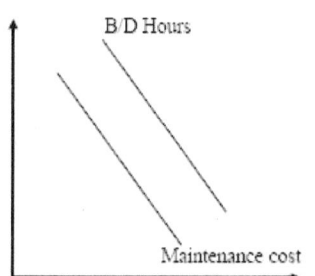
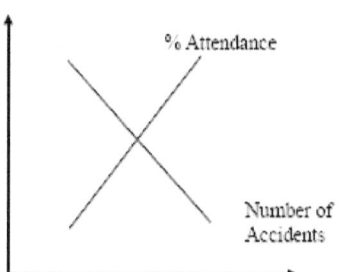
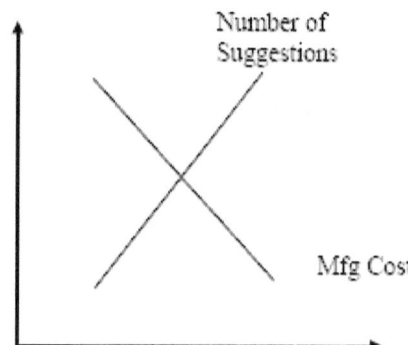
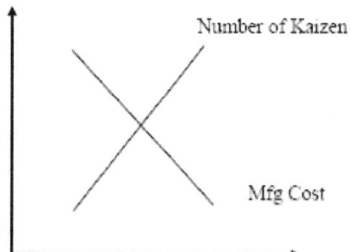
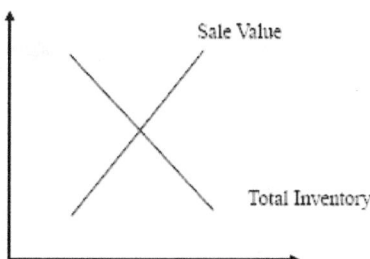

Cost Optimisation

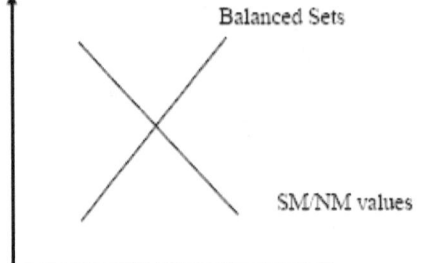

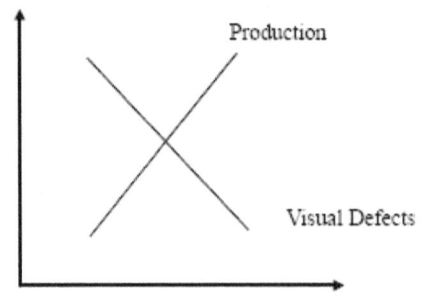

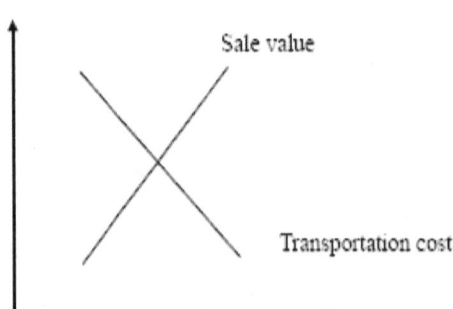

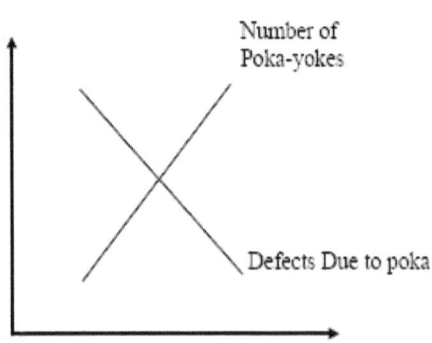

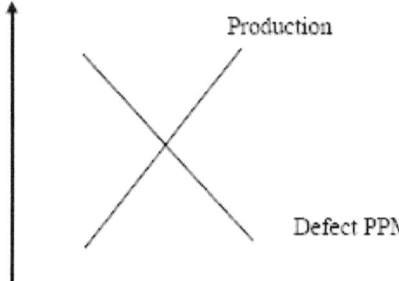

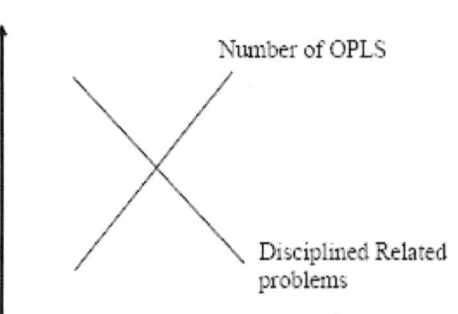

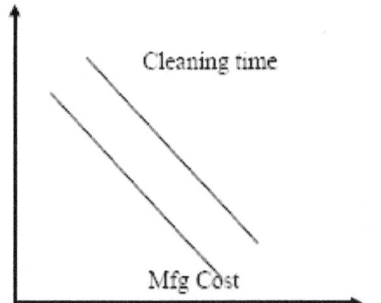

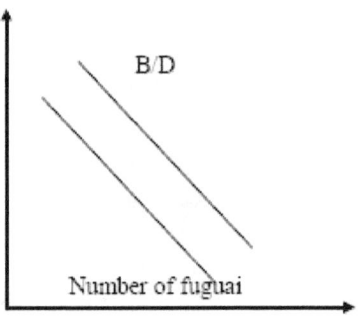

50 | Cost Optimisation

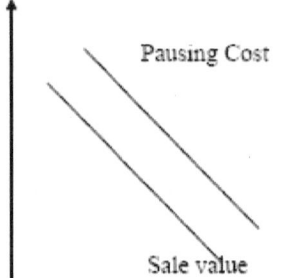

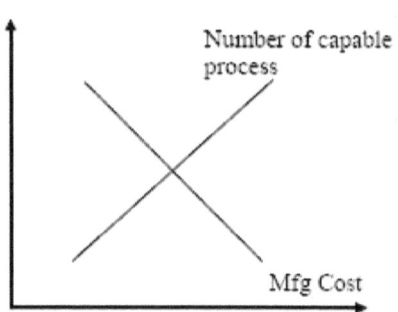

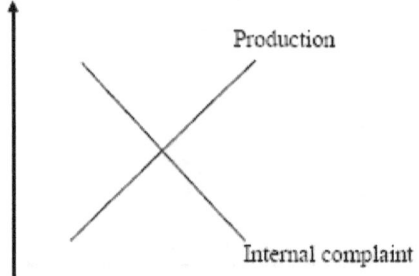

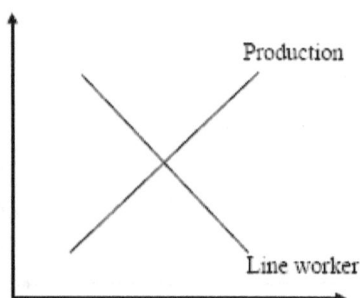

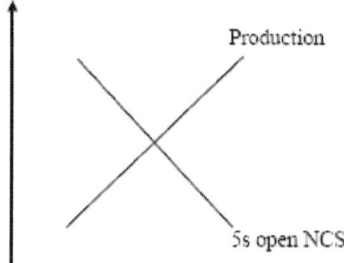
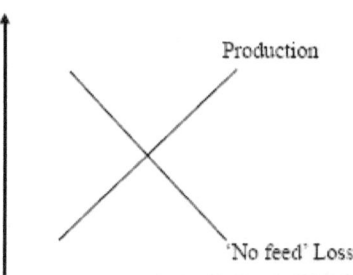
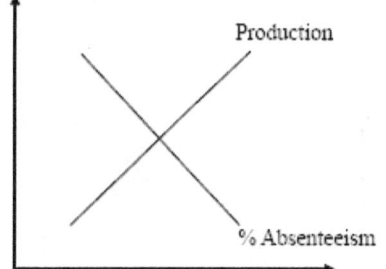
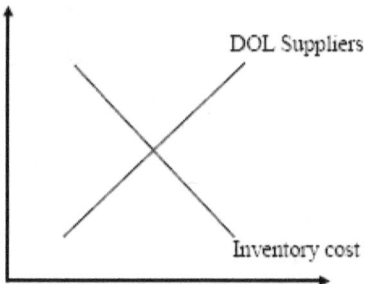

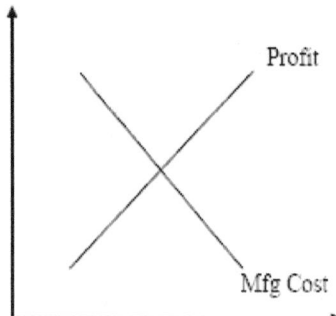
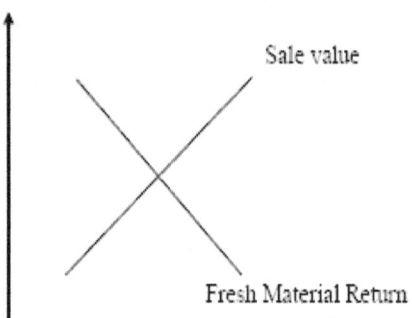

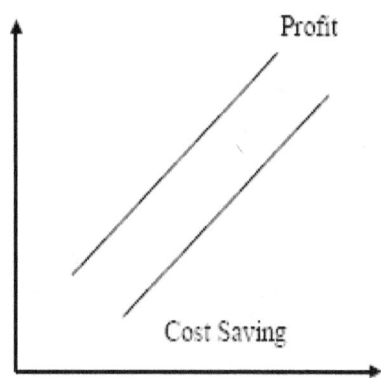

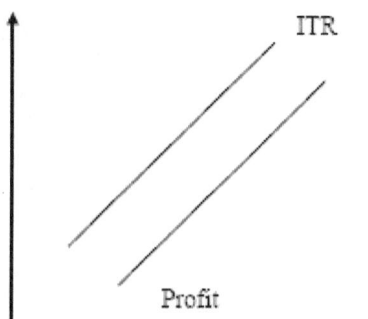
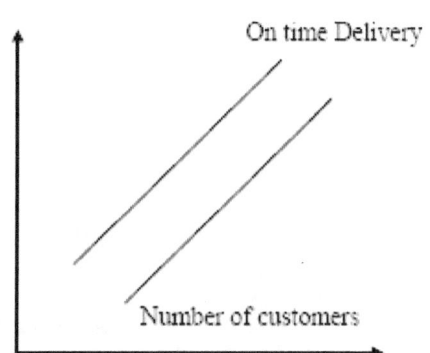
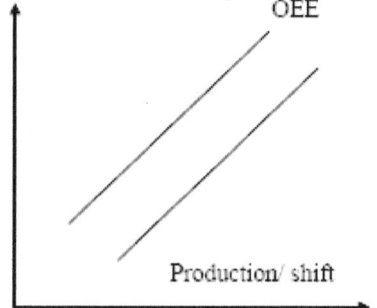
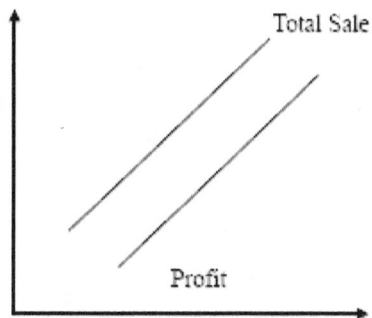

54 | Cost Optimisation

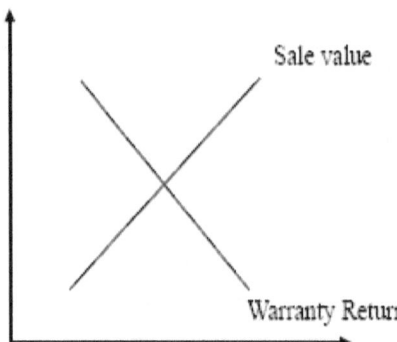

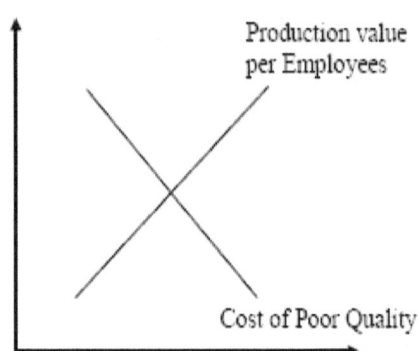

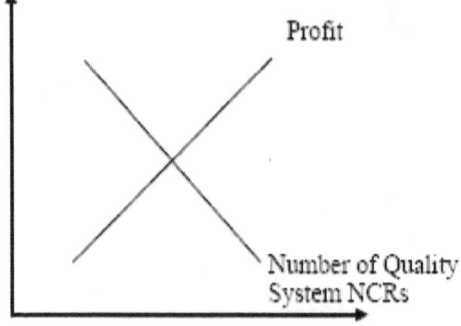

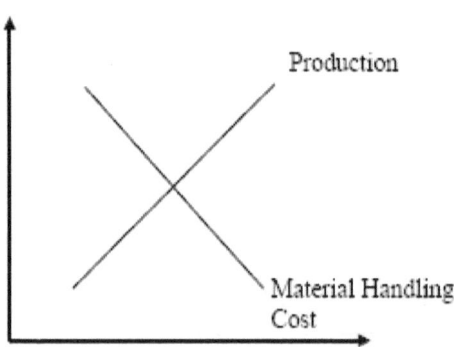

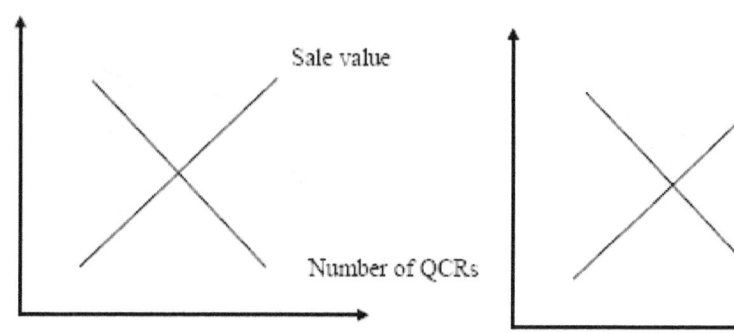

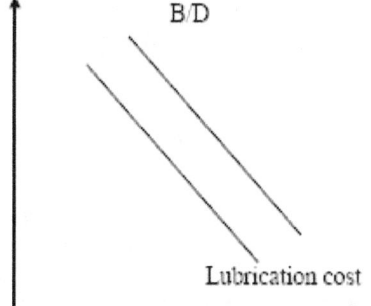

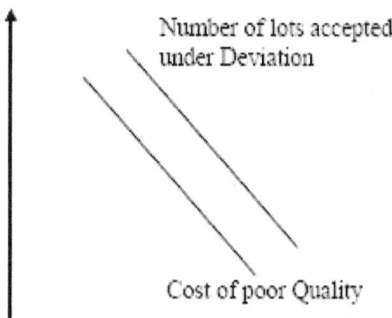

56 | Cost Optimisation

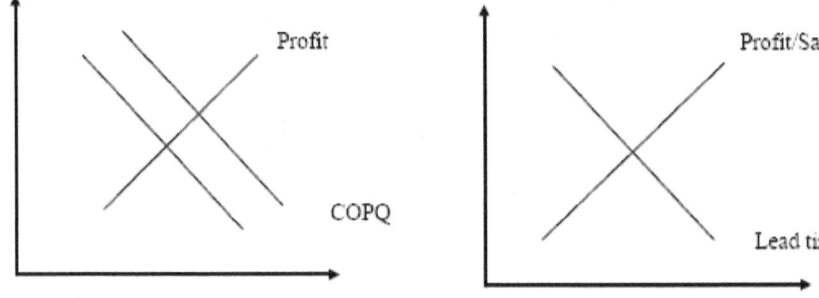

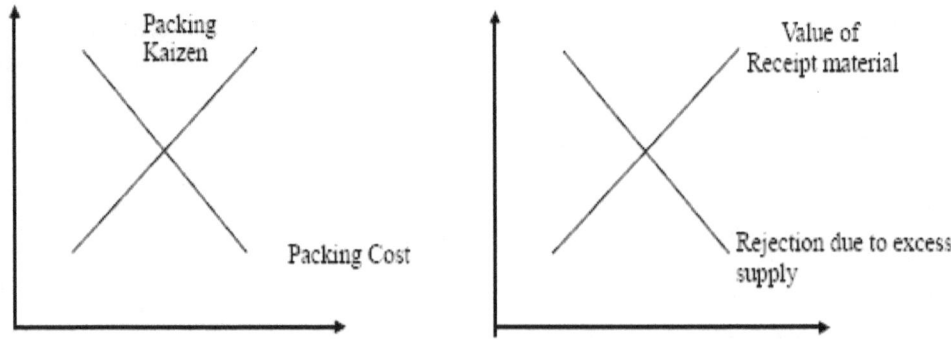

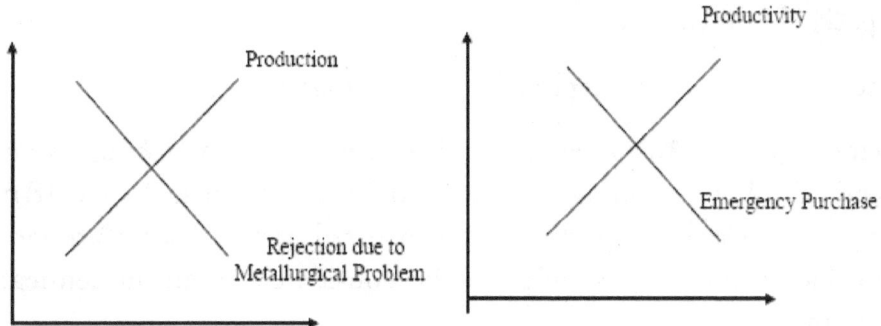

Motor Rating vs Energy Cost

After analysis, if we find, in place of 5 HP motor, the same amount of work with good quality can be achieved by 3/2 HP motor then replacement of higher HP shall be beneficial in energy cost reduction project.

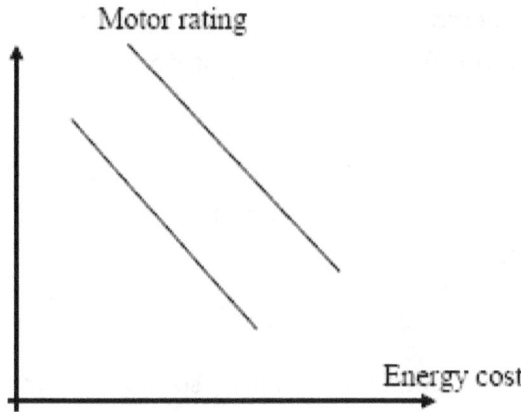

Aspects of Cost Control

There are mainly three types of aspects, as follows:

Planning: A set of target is established in the form of budgets and standards. This planning should be on authentic data based. If no supportive research reports, if not supported with at least 12 months data based, planning should not be considered as an authenticate planning.

Why?

Because, either manufacturability or sale ability both depends upon weather fluctuations, geometric conditions, shift and days conditions. Saturday's production quality is different from other day and vice versa rainy season has many bad effects on product quality.

Communication: To whom and why?

The main objective of this step of aspect is, right & authentic communications to right persons at right time but how will you believe on right person?

All that glitters are not gold. There are few ghosts & spy employees always exist in every old organization and those are not fit for any continual projects.

Yes, I do agree. Spy is to be avoided.

But clear cut communication is why so important?

Because, if they don't know the right situation then it will be highly ineffective for setting objective.

Motivation: is defined as the process that initiates, guides and maintains goal oriented behavior.

Everyone understands the benefits of cost optimization and we have seen in the beginning of this book also that profit is inversely proportion to total cost. When total cost decreases, profit increases. When cost will decrease then sales price will also decrease which will directly support in increase in sales resulted improvement in profitability, improvement in competitiveness. Our brand image will be bigger than others.

But,

I have met much top management and as per their views, they feel following disadvantages in such optimization drive in industries:

- It reduces the flexibility and process in a company.
- Restriction on innovation.

Requirement of Skillful & Experienced Personnel to Set the Standards

The main objective of cost optimization should be improvement in sales as much as possible. Manpower reduction should be the last option because a good team will be assets for any organization. We must utilize their experience, dedication & devotion in such creative way so that we can be able to increase sales volumes. Retaining good talents should be out first goal, if we want to maintain consistency and continuity in our overall performance.

Someone will tell that "SKILL can be bought once again."

But, you know well "PASSION can't be purchased!"

We know, teaching and preaching for cost reduction drive is easy but its implementation in any firm/business is difficult and main challenging point is to sustain at reduced standard.

The most difficult part of this journey is continual reduction till optimization and yes, the benchmarking standards are also in improving trends (Continual reduction).

Here I want to share one real small story.

When TPM activity started in north India (early 90's), I was representing as a coordinator for one company. Prof, Sueo Yamaguchi san was our mentor and as per prefixed scheduled plan, every month we get an opportunity to visit other cluster companies. Here case studies were for standardization of coolant changing frequency. Every company having their own standards. Mostly were following weekly coolant changing frequency without considering uses & conditions.

During study, final outcome established after 8 months that "Coolant changing frequency can be reduced to quarterly basis. Yes, for achieving those levels, many kaizen were completed including Ganga Flow, Chips management, improvement in filtration methods, filter quality, type and grade of coolant, required additive, some intermediate tests etc.

That company who had set the benchmark for coolant changing frequency on quarterly basis, after 2 years of detail study, they has beaten their own set target from 3 months to 6 months. This is called "Real Continual Improvement."

Few companies insisted that cost control in India is not possible because-Raw material cost is very high, power shortage especially in summer and rainy season, underutilization of available capacity, delay in issue of any license and high rates of taxes tend to raise the overall costs of production.

But, all these excuses are neither beneficial for the company and nor for the nations. We have seen the methodology and tools for cost savings. We can save huge by elimination of wastages, reduction of cost of poor quality, increasing of our internal efficiency, arresting of leakages an so no.

Features of Cost Reductions

Cost reduction is not concerned with setting targets and standards. Cost reduction is the final result in the cost control process.

We generally confused that cost control; cost cutting, cost reduction, cost optimization and cost standardization are same or different.

Answer is—different. Sequence would be:

- **Cost cutting**
- **Cost reduction**
- **Cost optimization**
- **Cost control**
- **Cost benchmarking**

Cost cutting means eliminate those expenses which are purely non-value added (like beer allowance during customer visit, leakages, Delay in unwanted material disposal).

Cost reduction means reduce excess consumptions.

Cost optimization means reach to optimum position, after that point reduction will affect the efficiency, quality & life of products/services.

Cost control means monitor the set consumption target.

Cost benchmarking means; establish new consumption standards by improvement in design, grade and methods.

So, now there should not be any further confusion from here.

Cost reduction will help in improving the set standards. It is a continuous, dynamic and innovative in nature, looking always for measures and alternatives to reduce costs. Although it is a corrective function but after it is helpful for starving new standards. This is applicable to every business activities. The major benefits are, it adds thinking and analysis to action at all levels of management.

Stages in Cost Reduction

- Cost cutting
- Cost management
- Cost design
- Cost positioning

Actually cost addition activities starts from product design stage itself. It is very important to understand that product development determines 80% of overall product cost. Wise company always invests more in design, development and R&D set up. Innovative design gives extra edge to win the new market & new customer.

One real example from my professional career, which I have seen very closely. There was one part number of truck application clutches. Warranty level was very high and customers were highly dissatisfied. During these struggling periods, customer has introduced one new supplier with low percentage of supply share. We visited along with team many times but unable to reach at real root cause. Finally we started visiting to local mechanics. We collected their observations very patiently and after 9 days of rigorous efforts, one clue observed in 21 defective pieces out of 27 pieces. Inner window of counter discs were breaking in all pieces at same locations.

We returned back from there and started deep analysis of window profile. Radius profile improved based on observations and parallel increased the chamfering of both ends. Made 10 samples and tested for full testing rigs. A small lot of 50 numbers finally fitted in vehicles. Finally, life of product improved by 62%.

Product life increased, means that product turned our balance sheet in huge profitability.

Profit Vs Profitability

Profit = Total revenue–Total costs

Profitability = Rate of return

Return on sales = Profit/Total revenue

Cost is controllable at design stage because at this stage we can,

- Design for manufacturing tools & dies
- Design for quality
- Design for lean

Lean manufacturing improves throughput by 90%, if implemented scientifically and systematically.

Every firm/business has a Value chain. We all work towards improving value chain.

Value Chains

- Primary activities:
  - Design
  - Research & development
  - Production
  - Marketing
  - Sales & service

- Support activities:
  - Material management
  - Human resources
  - Information system
  - Company infrastructure

Value Creation

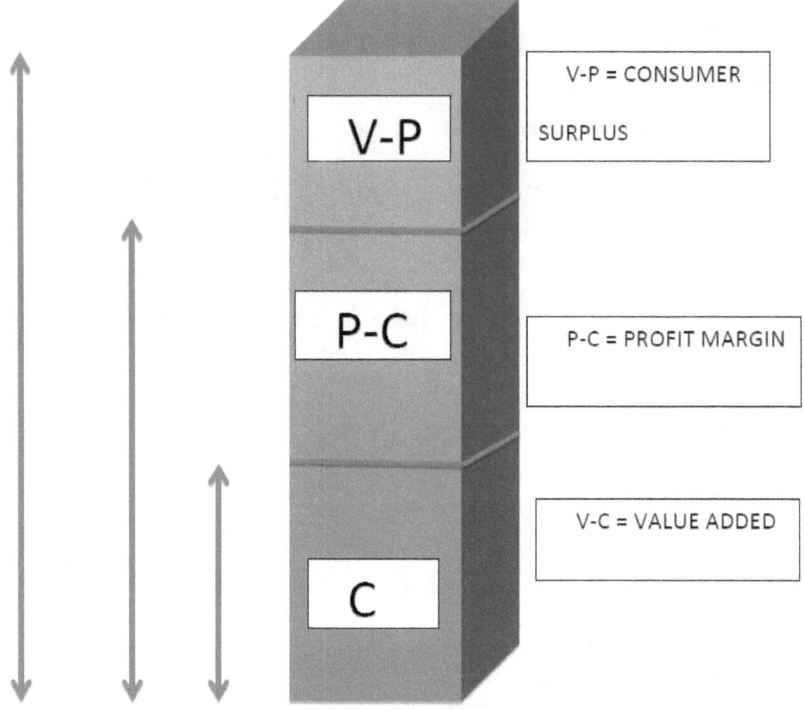

V = Consumer value

P = Market price

C = Cost of Production

The Cost Structure

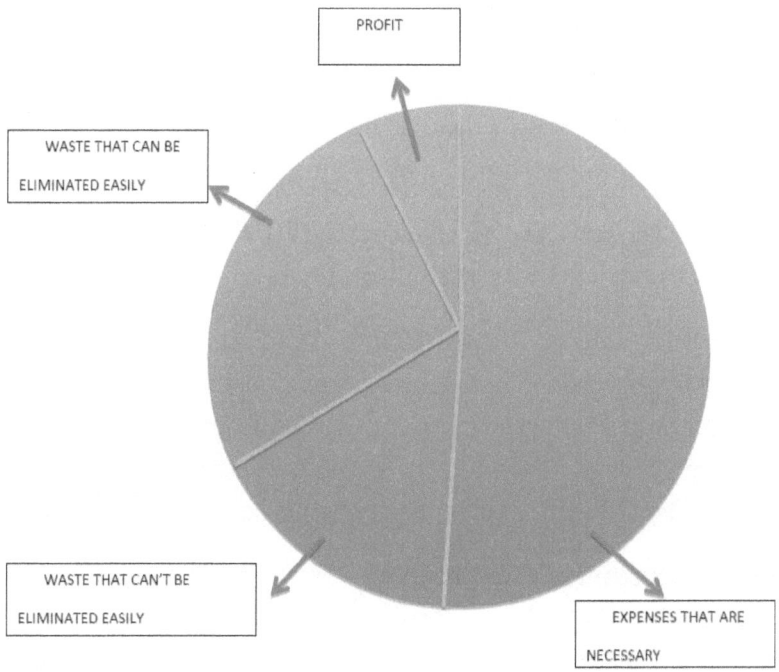

Generally most of the companies spend a lot of time trying to reduce costs mainly focusing on:

- Negotiating down material prices
- Limiting salary rises
- Pushing the employees to work hard for long hours

What they don't realize is, these are not the major cost drivers!

What can really bring costs down by 15–25% after one year of reorganization?

- Simplifying the flow of materials through different processes
- Improving the way each process step is conducted

The key is to eliminate as much waste as possible.

We will discuss in brief about "Waste that can be eliminated easily" as follows. We all know, eliminating waste **completely** is virtually impossible but a good part of it, can be eliminated **easily**.

These "7 Wastes" can be reduced by 70–90% within one year, if really worked systematically with disciplined approach.

Transportation: Moving materials or products from one place to another, simply because the different steps of a production are not side by side. Such types of wastes are easily visible in old plant or mostly SMEs. They generally follow process oriented layout or they keep any machine side by side without much focusing on operational sequence.

Suppose customer has ordered one product which required punching, machining, heat treatment, surface treatment, sub assembly, final assembly, packing and packaging before dispatch to customer. To reduce transportation losses, one can make cellular layout. Pre-kitting is also an option where heat treatment process is involved.

Inventory: It starts from planning stage. Production planning team can play a big role in optimization of inventory through real data based projections to manufacturing department/purchase department. There are mainly 3 types of inventory called as "GREEN INVENTORY (Runner), GREY INVENTORY (Repeater) & RED INVENTORY (stranger)." Green inventory is being considered as big asset for any manufacturing plant whereas grey and red inventories are liabilities for plant. Grey inventory is due to over production, safety stock, and order cancellation. Red inventory is the worst for any plant, which are on hold since long may be due to inferior quality or obsolete order quantity due to design or any other features changes.

The company's cash is tied up in inventory that sits still most of the time and that necessitates lots of warehousing space.

Motion: Every walking is not value addition and those steps which are not for value addition; customer will not pay for that. It means the process steps that don't add value to the product, such as walking to pick a bin of products or going to see the dies status at tool room or searching the setting blocks. All these are cost addition activities and certainly not value addition. Excessive motion losses are due to bad 5S and poor operation's layout. Bending and stretching to pick up parts are visual examples of motion losses present in any manufacturing line.

Waiting: Waiting is one type of time losses. The famous proverbs we all know that time is money so time losses means money losses, resulted profit reduction.

Operators who can't work because they are waiting for materials or because their machine has broken down; products waiting for weeks in a queue. Some common waiting losses are:

- Operators waiting for material
- Waiting for material
- Waiting for correct machine
- Waiting for first piece approval
- Waiting for calibrated instrument/gauges
- Waiting for related SOPs & OPLs (One point lessons)
- Waiting for setting
- Waiting for next operation
- Waiting for light

Over production: categorised as the worst wastes because our business objective is to increase sales but in case of over production means made more than customer demand. Generally plant managers utilize their workmen time for producing more without balancing next operations. Why it is treated as the worst waste because till that position we have invested time, money and efforts but we are not able to sell those quantities to recover our invested resources. It might stay in inventory for a long time and lose value.

Over processing: Spending sometimes/energy that is not necessary during a process (may be due to no work instructions exists, maybe there are not adequate, or maybe they are not respected,). Over processing is also due to not meeting the drawing specifications in previous operations and the current operation is to maintain that balance gaps. General examples of such operations are de-burring, de-flashing.

Defects: Product quality that is not meeting customer's requirement. Some out of specification products can be made correct after rectification is called rework. This extra operation is cost addition which should be eliminated by acting on real root cause. Some pieces are beyond rectifications and useless of the customer. The big loss.

Cost Saving Policy

We continually reduce our manufacturing costs by identifying the production constraints (manufacturing bottleneck) and then applying all the related tools and techniques at our disposal to improve the performance of the bottleneck. When it is no longer constraint then we identify new constraint and repeat. Tools and techniques including the past proven best practices from Lean manufacturing, Theory of constraints, TPM, Six sigma and 5S. Non-constraint reductions in costs are also valued, but are a second priority for eliminating wastes and increasing throughput at the constraint.

We will discuss those manufacturing best practices in details which are very essential, effective and efficient methods for cost optimization.

For Cost saving ideas sharing, we will categorise the potential areas first and then under each category we will discuss all those potential possibilities.

Best Practices in Manufacturing to Reduce Unwanted Costs

- 5S
- Single piece flow
- Kaizen culture
- TPM
- TQM
- TOC
- TCM
- Kanban
- JIT
- LEAN manufacturing
- 6 Sigma
- LEAN 6 –sigma
- SMED
- POKA-YOKE
- 8D
- QMS
- Zero Defect
- FMEA

All the above mentioned tools and techniques are for profit maximization by reducing and/or eliminating unwanted costs.

Theory of Constraints (TOC)

Theory of constraints (TOC) identifies the most important limiting factor that stands in the way of achieving a goal (such as making a profit) and then systematically involves that constraint until it is no longer the limiting factor. In manufacturing processes the constraint is often referred as a bottleneck. Interestingly, the constraint is not necessarily equipment. It can also be policy, paradigm or even the market place.

The underlying power of TOC flows from its laser like focus on a single goal (Profit) and systematically removing impediments to achieving more of that goal. From the perspective of reducing costs, one of the most appealing characteristics of Theory of Constraints is that it inherently prioritizes and focuses improvement activities where they will have the greatest cost impact; the constraint.

The Experience Curve

Potential Areas for Cost Savings

- Design & Development
- Procurement
- Materials
- Material Handling
- Maintenance
- Processing
- Quality
- Communication
- Advertisement
- Sales & Marketing
- Energy consumption
- Consumables
- Insurance

REDUCTIONS for PROFIT MAXIMISATION!

1. Cycle time
2. Throughput time
3. TAKT time management
4. Lead time
5. Planning time

6. Design & development time
7. Inspection & testing time
8. Product verification & validation time
9. Field trial time
10. Customer complaints handling time
11. Rework time
12. Procurement time
13. Processing time
14. Cleaning time
15. Lubrication time
16. Tightening time
17. Adjustment time
18. Setup time
19. Meeting time
20. Traveling time
21. Walking time
22. Material handling time
23. Approval time
24. Disposal time
25. Idle time
26. Replacement time
27. Re-fitting time
28. Sweeping time
29. Parking time
30. Marking time
31. Printing time
32. Erasing time
33. Gauging time
34. Engaging time
35. Review/Revision time
36. Overheating time
37. Cooling time
38. Settling time

39. Fettling time
40. Deburring time
41. Shifting time
42. Decision making time
43. Response time
44. First piece approval time
45. Packing time
46. Dispatching time
47. Labelling time
48. Waiting time
49. Opening & closing time
50. Increments delay time
51. Searching time

We can take as quantifiable monitoring projects to reduce above mentioned FATS to improve our plant's profitability!

It will be very effective KRA towards TEI (Total Employees Involvement)

INCREASE for PROFIT MAXIMISATION!

1. Numbers of positive people
2. Numbers of energy efficient machines
3. Numbers of SOPs for each process
4. Numbers of training hours
5. Numbers of Kaizen competitions
6. Numbers of Poka-yokes
7. Numbers of DOL suppliers
8. Numbers of attribute gauges
9. Numbers of digital measuring instruments
10. Numbers of QCCs/SGIA teams
11. Increase total employees engagement
12. Increase 5S score
13. Increase numbers of capable processes

14. Increase MY machine concepts
15. Increase JH practices
16. Counted without counting storage
17. Increase numbers of wheeled trolley
18. Increase GANGA FLOW machining Operations
19. Increase cleaned without cleaning operations
20. Increase lux level of the plant
21. Increase auto lubrication mechanism
22. Increase numbers of HOME DOCTORS concepts
23. Increase numbers of digital displays
24. Numbers of de-skilled processes
25. Numbers of safety sensors
26. Dial indicators to digital indicators
27. Increase FMEA correctness
28. Increase standardisation of nuts & bolts
29. Increase possibilities of day lighting
30. Increase use of solar energy
31. Increase standardised painting
32. Vibration pads below machine base
33. Increase numbers of U-Shape layouts
34. Numbers of multi-skilled operators
35. Increase transparency in panels

Some Implementation TIPS

START recording & monitoring, improvement will start!

START calling your employees, & ask him: why are you not happy today? All is well?

His dedication towards company will improve!

START taking lunch in canteen, food quality will improve!

START process audit randomly, product quality will improve!

STICK to weekly disposal of scrap, employees' participation will improve!

SEND birthday card to your employees, loyalty will improve!

INTRODUCE GAME in company, teamwork will improve!

Start something from today and continually adds every week, PROFITABILITY will improve!!

Save Cost Through Capable Processes

Acceptance Criteria

Acceptance criteria for critical vs. non-critical characteristics

	Short-term	Long-term	Decision
Red (Bad)	<1.33	<1.00	
Yellow (Marginal)	1.33-1.67	1.00-1.33	
Green (Good)	>1.67	>1.33	

Cpk must be greater than or equal to 1.67 for critical processes

Cpk must be greater than or equal to 1.33 for non-critical processes

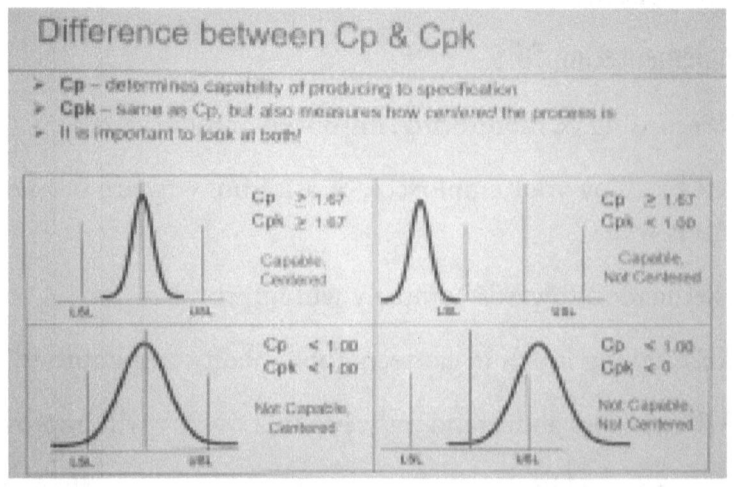

Difference between Cp & Cpk

- **Cp** – determines capability of producing to specification
- **Cpk** – same as Cp, but also measures how centered the process is
- It is important to look at both!

Industries Wishes!

Highest productivity, zero defects, No customer returns/complaints, lowest mfg cost, JIT inventory, 100% On time delivery, safe, clean green factory with OLD WORKING CULTURE!

OLD CULTURE = One man army, spy driven, no 5S as working culture, Many improvements at one machine, modern testing machine with outdated mfg machine, no documented & approved policy, QMS certificate for customers, very few pampered employees, tall target with no celebration, improvement means cost reduction, high temperatures/high humidity/dirty &dry heat treatment shop, multi-locational scrap yards, in one man =many men, Training means cost addition, paperless company means no recording of accidents, dirty & stinky workers toilet!

Wishes = Dream

Culture = Reality!

Not matching but we want top rated profitability.

Why Consultant?

YOU ARE GOOD, YOU CAN BE BETTER,

IF THE BEST IS POSSIBLE, TRY TO BECOME GREAT: MISSION OF EXCELLENT BUSINESS GROUP!

A consultant is not the master of your products even not carrying extraordinary knowledge of the technology then why consultants are needed for growth & Sustenance of Improvement culture in the Plant??

A good consultant is unbiased, non-political, fearless, systematic, disciplined, curious, analytical approach, good observant, experienced of different working processes & working cultures, carrying many success stories; many turn arounds, many types of team building tactics, different types of performance measuring & monitoring systems.

A good consultant is extending his hands to share experiences with you by interaction, implementation of WCM system at your plant with your team, robust SOPs & Training. So Many ideas.

Road map-Documentation-Visit of plant-Developing change agents from your team-guiding-Reviewing the progress-presenting the facts & figures-Results-Celebration-All around motivation-cultural change for Sustenance-safe, clean & green company-all will happen-finally Plant will get sustainable profit!

BUT IT WILNOT BE POSSIBLE WITHOUT YOUR COMMITMENT & INVOLVEMENT! MATCH THE SPEED W/O ARGUMENTS!

Productivity = Output/Input

Productivity is the ratio & we know ratio has no unit but has own limit. Reduction in denominator gives increase in output but the key is—❓how much reduction and at which ingredient? These answers required experience/expertise and not speed. "HOW MUCH" & "AT WHICH" these are key deciding factors for growth and branding of any plants, slightly mistakes can shake the whole foundation (Balance sheet & Branding image).

Why we need experienced persons in our plant? Answer is: to get right answer of " how much & at which." I have seen many companies have become new bench mark for the industry and many have shut down too. Very few are experts, who really know the difference between "investment Vs Expenses." Very important and sensitive points. Making more is not the business goal but selling more at good price is.

You cannot/shouldn't reduce manpower from a certain limit; you cannot keep motivation at denominator. Experienced people can give you right direction and right decision for denominator. Nominators are the result, not process. In depth knowledge of denominator is the key for making profitable company.

Speed is required but in which direction is the crucial point. Speed required more numbers but direction required rich experience.

Think wisely!

Plant Quality: Gate, Toilet, Canteen & Scrap Yard!

Quality is an intention. Sophisticated & advanced measuring instruments are cost additions because our intention towards quality is dual/subjective/controversial/mood based/link based/time based. Different quality for same products for different customers/segments. We make different quality in day and in night.

Market is customer centric. Competition is very high. Still most of the companies face the problem of poor quality, In spite of various quality models, processes; the issue of poor quality is there. Why it is so?

Answer is simple: Our dual policy, our attitude, our intention are not good. We are capable but not stable & predictable. In presence of Top management (during day), our quality is top class but in his absence…? Night shift…? When specialists workmen are on leave…?

Why I am repeating "intention" many times in this post?

Kindly tell me, have we uniform system at gate for all and for always?

Our toilet quality for staffs & workmen are same?

Our food quality is highly hygienic and same food for all?

Our scrap yard is being monitored on daily basis by quality head to eliminate these problems systematically? With application of different tools & techniques? Our manual filling data are authentic? "NO".

Resources & Satisfaction of SMEs

What should be real business objectives?

Manufacturing & selling of products? Designing & selling of services? Spending less & getting more? Feeling financially satisfied? Getting better social status?

But in my views: Business objective should be "Making safe & happy society!" Safe = mentally, physically, emotionally, socially & nationally! Society = Customers, employees, employers, environment& citizens

We, all know, the satisfaction level varies with person to person, society to society, locations to locations. SMEs have bigger dream, short term vision, limited resources, Inadequate planning capability & localised actions. All 5 are not matching so always finding difficulties in survival & growth. They always prefer inferior quality RM (cheaper), less manpower, short cut localised processes to make more. Actual balancing of demands & production are not there, resulted higher unwanted inventory, more procurement, higher rejections, low yield, higher mfg cost, unsafe actions & conditions, higher repair & maintenance cost, lower working efficiency, dissatisfied customers & employees and lower profits. All are unsafe & unhappy.

Then, what should be done?

Smaller investment, SOPs, KRA, 5S culture, demand = production & good positive manpower!

"SPC" of "Business"

SPC = Processes those are (S) stable shall be mostly (P) predictable and (C) capable. Stability is the key criteria for the (R) reliability of any individual, team and processes.

But, the vital question is – how stability can be achieved? Without stability, characters of any individual, team or processes cannot be predictable. We can't believe on the capability of any individual/processes which are not predictable.

Process average (X-bar) is important but range (R)/Variation (standard deviations) are more important than that. Range is the indicator of characters of any individual/processes.

Stability depends on character. Variations in characters are the law of nature. It can be reduced but can't be eliminated. For controlling characters, we must identify those behaviours which generally effects on it like settings, dating, temptations, vibrations, experts/beginners, day/night, loose/tight, dark/bright, dry/wet, measuring devices, hot/cold.

We must establish predictable patterns of variations and it will depend on correct methods of sampling before talking to whole populations.

Range of individual character can badly effect on balance sheets (process capability or Profitability of business). Control the standard deviations more rightly and tightly

Challenges for SME's!

No one wants to die early, everyone wants happy and long life everyone is trying for the best fit. After GST introduction, life of non-systematic companies is not the same as earlier. Introduction of good system requires some initial investment in the form of time & money.

As per Industries data, if systematic 5S can be done for 3 months then a good improvement in productivity, quality and cost reduction are clearly visible in balance sheet (honesty/transparently). Now the crucial challenges start from here, because these 3 months journey has driven by consultant and now for longevity, this system should be established as working culture by the management and employees of the Plant. Some challenges:

1. Lack of good coordinator.
2. Don't want to invest in communication system.
3. Hard to find replacement of non-performer due to long association.
4. Avoid investing on basic infrastructure.
5. They don't want to implement suggestion scheme.
6. After target hitting, they don't want to give credit and parallel motivation.
7. They avoid transparency in data sharing especially sales figures and purchasing.
8. They consider Kaizen as cost.
9. Want to keep more inventories due to different fears.
10. Different treatment for sales & Operations.

Cost: The Ghost

- Use of excessive Raw material.
- Higher rate of purchase of RM.
- Poor/unbalanced procurement planning.
- High rework % age with existing process.
- High rejection % age with existing process.
- Rejection/rework more due to skipping from approved SOP.
- Lack of process audit by experienced engineer/manager.
- Expenses in customer complaints handling.
- Multiple materials handling within plant.
- Double/multiple touching of materials for the same operations.
- Selection of poor capability of suppliers (considered only lower cost, not quality).
- Deployment of excessive manpower.
- Appointment & retention of negative attitude manpower.
- Continuation with low efficiency manpower.
- Continuation with physically unfit manpower.
- Low experience & unskilled manpower.
- Absenteeism more than 3% of the plant.
- Presence of various types of leakages: Water, oil, coolant, air, secret information's.
- Low productivity compared to rated machine capacity.
- Huge unwanted production (Production not as per customer demands/Push system production/Over production).
- Unplanned & Unexpected machine breakdown resulted whole line stoppage.
- Initial start-up losses (Beginning of the shift).
- Minor stoppages during processes.
- Material/tool/documents searching time more.
- More waiting time for correct man/machine/material.
- Poor storage area (full of dusts, overheat, more moisture).
- High set up time.
- Bigger batch sizes of production.

- Low yield.
- Long walking distance due to poor layout.
- Manual material handling.
- Higher repair & maintenance cost.
- Frequent repair & maintenance needed due to misalignments.
- Huge grey & red inventory.
- Higher green inventory.
- Material kept more than 5 feet height.
- Material kept in rack and pallets (slow movement/extra efforts for picking & handling).
- Wrong process sequence.
- Procedure for 100% visual inspection by same person on daily basis.
- Short cut in operation cycle time.
- High & low temperature in heat treatment operation.
- High & low pressure in mfg & testing of products.
- Poor lighting in shop floor especially near inspection point.
- Noisy working environment.
- Poor tool design & management.
- Dirty & dangerous heat treatment shop.
- Procurement of robots/fully automatic machine without line balancing.
- No low cost automation in the plant for monotonous job.
- Low VAPCO due to negative attitude.
- Low inventory turnover ratio.
- Unhealthy working environment (dark, dry, hot, humid, slippery, smoky).
- Untrained casual workmen at critical operation.
- Taking out multi pages coloured prints for internal uses.
- Unsafe actions in the plant.
- Unsafe conditions in the plant.
- Disposal of unwanted materials at low price (No policy for 3 quotations).
- Over writing/no highlighting of critical information.

- Delay disposal of unwanted materials.
- No disposal of unwanted machines/materials.
- Unavailability of SOPs.
- Idle running of machines.
- Low process capability of machines.
- Multiple inspections/over quality.
- Low life of machine spare parts (Genuine spares).
- High variations in repeatability & reproducibility (R&R).
- Frequent power failure & no back up of CNC machines.
- Culture of low talent retention.
- Lack of regular & proper cleaning of machines (not only outer body of machine).
- Lack of lubrication of rotating & sliding parts.
- Manual checking of variable parameters with mechanical instruments for accuracy.
- Use of low grade lubricating oils (not as per specified grades).
- Premature failure of products at customer end/field.
- Dissatisfied customers.
- Dissatisfied employees.
- Dissatisfied suppliers.
- High consumable consumptions.

Some Cost Saving Ideas for Medium and Big Business

❖ **At design stage**

- Cost reduction through design improvement can result in significant product cost saving, manufacturing cost saving and life cycle cost saving.
- Design for manufacturability: how to use concurrent engineering to rapidly develop low cost and high quality products at the cheapest cost for lean production.
- During designing, we have come across at many design options to meet the final product's characteristics but only one will be the lowest cost option.

- Develop that in half the time with these principles:
  - Product development determines 80% of product cost.
  - The concept phase alone determines 60% of cost.
  - Practice concurrent engineering with early and active participation of manufacturing, purchase, design, engineering and vendors.
  - Implement design for manufacturability (DFM), design for lean and design for quality (DFQ).
  - Concurrent engineering with manufacturing ensures the best teamwork, avoid distant offshoring.
  - If outsourcing is required then kindly choose local vendors participation in product development teams.
  - But only select that vendors who can help during development process by giving priority for loading & processing of your products and can communicate development status without any reminder,
  - Implement standardisation and good product portfolio for the best focus.
  - Total cost measurements to quantify all costs affected by design.

❖ **Material Costs**
- Procure at less rate
- Use less
- Purchase materials in bulk to drive down unit cost.
- This bulk purchase decision should be purely on consumption pattern base. If you are using large quantity, go for bulk. If you use less quantity, kindly don't go for bulk. As a small business owner, you could greatly reduce their expenses by buying only what you need today, not what you think, you will need for future. Focus should be to improve cash flow.
- Yes, there may be chance when you need unique composition or feature raw material and supplier is far away from your plant then there is good consideration to go for bulk purchase.

- Research and determine the right type of materials required for your purpose, without compromising with quality and life of end products.
- If features are not vital to the function or quality of your goods, then you can go for de-graded material with full monitoring control from receipt to dispatch. Inspection and testing frequency in such cases to be increased to ensure required quality material dispatches to customer's end.
- For proper control of consumptions, SOPs for all operations are mandatory because rejection or deviation from desired quality will lead to more consumption.
- Ensuring for tight controls, periodical required training to be imparted to all related employees.
- Initial setup rejection is too high. Setup methodology to be improved.

   In plastic mfg. industries, it contributes nearly 72% of total % of rejection and similar in case of sheet metal components mfg sector.

   Sometimes such initial rejections noticed at heat treatment plant too.

- Robust tooling to reduce the amount of materials scrapped during production.
- Damages during material handling also increase material costs.
- Quality deterioration during transportation, resulted scrap generation which finally leads too high consumptions for lower output.
- Wrong CNC programming
- Low yield tool design especially in sheet metal where pins & slots provisioning considered into calculations.
- Wrong set up during shearing of sheets (More wastage as called end pieces).
- Higher clearance in moulds resulted more unwanted flashes. Over processing "De-flashing" also added to rectify this and

finally it is counted as an additional required operation. We know, customer will not pay for it, so it is purely cost addition due to wastage of materials.
- 5S, LEAN manufacturing, FMEA and 6-Sigma tools and techniques to be implemented systematically.
- Expert's assistance can be taken for better results.
- Scrap management
- DOL (Direct on line)
- Make and buy decision

❖ Labour Costs

- If physical labour is the biggest expenses in manufacturing your products then controlling labour costs will give you the quickest path to increased profit.
- Either you appoint low cost employee or make them more efficient.
- It can be obtained by employing fresher/unskilled labour and then train them as per your needs.
- Study the production practices and eliminate the wasted steps in the process.
- Walking is not equal to working. Simply walking is the cost addition to the product.
- Cycle time reduction can be done by providing specialized training that allows employees to work at a faster pace.
- Offer incentives to employees who can introduce labour saving techniques to your production facility.
- If you run a low-margin labour intensive business, such as restaurant, labour is likely to be a huge cost consideration for you. Such companies must pay careful attention to local minimum wages and overtime regulations.
- Pool resources with other small business:
    - Buying group
    - Cooperatives

- ➤ Resource libraries
- ➤ partner network
- ➤ Trade association and local business network

❖ **Production Cost**

- Lean manufacturing relentlessly eliminates waste from manufacturing where waste is defined as any activity that does not add value from the customer's perspective.
- The key requirements of lean production are product line rationalisation and standardisation which simplify both the supply chain and manufacturing operations.
- It provides a way to do more and more with less and less:
    - Less human efforts
    - Less equipment
    - Less time and
    - Less space

While coming closer and closer to providing customers with exactly

What they want.

- By implementation of Lean manufacturing,
    - Productivity can be increased up to 90% from earlier.
    - Reduction in throughput time by 80%
    - Inventory carrying cost reduction up to 80%
    - Cost of poor quality reduction by 50%
    - Accident reduction by 90%
    - Lead time reduction by 50%
    - Can offer a wider variety of products within product family, at very modest additional cost.
    - Reduce capital investments required to very modest levels (if facilities and equipment can be freed up or sold).
    - Manufacturing in batches drastically raises costs and lead times because of the following reasons:

- ✓ More space required
- ✓ High throughput time due to waiting at each stage.
- ✓ High WIP
- ✓ High defects
- ✓ Many disruptions
- ✓ Low flexibility

- Set up and batch elimination: if part variety is too excessive to allow distribution at all points of use, then enough parts for a batch must be assembled into a kit form, which is put together in the raw material warehouse, derived to the assembly area, and then distribution to part bins. This kitting is a setup which will inhibit flexibility.
- Tools & tooling setup:
  - Eliminate setup: design the products/processes to eliminate the need for tooling changes for cutting tools, dies, moulds, tool plates and fixtures.
  - Tool plates and fixtures can be designed to be versatile enough to accept a common blank which then can be customised.
  - By seeing the above mentioned both possibilities, if these are not possible then think for making set up changes as quickly as possible (SMED).
  - Consolidate inflexible parts: It should be designed to be versatile enough to accommodate all products that are supplied by each production machine.
- CNC setup time reduction:
  - Maximize the amount of dimensional variation done with CNC.
  - Standardize raw work pieces and fixturing to eliminate setup.
  - Quick and automatic program change.

- o Standard cutting tools within tool changing capability.
- o Automatic material feed and ejections.
- o For sheet metal, nesting optimization.
- The Lean supply chain: Just in time supply
- Track inventory closely: If you run an inventory based business, carrying less inventory means having less money tied up and more money in the bank. Begin inventory monitoring more closely to make sure you are not spending more than is really needed.
- Manually inventory management gives only 60% correctness even with involvement of huge manpower. We must go for some good inventory management software like ERP, SAP, and TATA Ion etc.
- In such types of software, accuracy is up to 98% with some authorization to use and consume or material losses during heated operations, deflating.
- By this software, we can take out various types of consumptions statistics along with comparative consumption patterns.
- Product identification and traceability becomes easy.
- Flow manufacturing/single piece flow production:
  - o It has a distinct advantage for assuring quality at the source.
  - o Flow manufacturing eliminates the possibility that recurring defects may be built into several batches before being caught at a downstream inspection step.
  - o People working in flow manufacturing look for any visible deviation as each part is handled to the next station.
  - o If the part does not fit or work in the next operation, the feedback will be immediate, leading to quick rectification of the problem.
- U-Shaped layout: This type of layout has an extra benefits like Visual control, everyone in the line can see the whole operation, enhancing visual control, thus resulting in greater

group ownership, Kaizen and problem solving actions. Visual control can be further enhanced with clearly visible Andon lights and product line performance display boards. We can add electronic display of machine working status with buzzer system and inventory control board with beep system. Such lay out emphasis on group performance over individual performance. Establishes good team work in the manufacturing system.

- o Multiskilling: U-shaped layout also advocates for introduction of multi-skilling culture because as discussed in previous bullets, U-shaped layout focuses on group achievement. In this case, when one or two operators shall be on leave then production of that line should not suffer due to unavailability of manpower. So automatically other operators get chance to learn other's work. It is win-win situation for both (Management and worker). Management gets on time correct output from that product line and operators get additional skills.
- o Multi-manning:
- o Multi-machining:
- o Problem Heard: Problems at all stations will be heard by the entire team, these leading to faster problem identification and restoration.
- o Helping out: If one worker gets behind, nearby worker can help him out, even end to beginning.
- o Skipping steps: Having work stations closer together, makes it easier to process orders that skip steps.

- Machine maintenance: In sequential single piece flow, when one production machine breaks down, the whole work line will go down. Therefore proactive equipment maintenance is important to prevent unexpected production interruptions. A good TPM program should ensure this.
- Line balancing: Ideally, to achieve optimal machine, tools and work station utilization, single piece flow lines should be

balanced so that the time to do the required tasks at each station, called the TAKT TIME, is fairly constant.

- o If TAKT TIME at each station = Work station capacity, arrange into sequential line.
- o If TAKT TIME is not equal to work station capacity, but does not vary with products then,
    - ✓ Find faster machines to achieve balance
    - ✓ Group machines/work stations into parallel paths to achieve better balance.
    - ✓ If underutilized machines are not expensive, don't worry about balancing to run/balance whole line.
- o If TAKT TIME varies with different products,
    - ✓ Make machine/operation flexible enough.
    - ✓ Sequence jobs to compensate for imbalances.
    - ✓ Size the line, based on the most expensive machine and provide excess capacity for the less expensive machine.

- Levelling production: Check for the customer demands for the month. These demands can be fulfilled in 25/26 working days (if not specified any special request by customer), so we can calculate per day required quantity after dividing month's total quantity by 25.

    Suppose customer demand = 10000 pcs
    Per day required quantity = 10000/25 = 400/day
    (Some company considers 20% of factor of safety, means they want to complete full quantity in 20 days).
    400/2 = 200 pieces/shift
    If line capacity based on the largest cycle time = 360/2 = 180,
    Then either overtime can be allowed or look for production on alternate line.

❖ **COPQ (Cost of poor quality) and COQ (Cost of quality)**

Cost of Quality

- The low hanging fruit in reducing the company's cost of quality, is to rationalize products to get rid of low-volume, low-profit products that get less kaizen focus and have less sophisticated tooling and procedures. Legacy products and spare parts may need to be eliminated or outsourced if they are not synergistic with the current generation of products. Infrequently built products would have higher cost of quality.

    o Designing in quality: the cost of quality begins with designing in quality to avoid:

    - ✓ costly defects,
    - ✓ Errors,
    - ✓ Rework,
    - ✓ Scrap,
    - ✓ Procurement of replacement materials,
    - ✓ Factory capacity degradation
    - ✓ Requalification,
    - ✓ Recertification costs and
    - ✓ Overheads demand to sort out quality problems

    Which robs resources from implementing the overall cost reduction strategy.

    For this,

    - ✓ Optimize the tolerances.
    - ✓ Refer past quality problems
    - ✓ Simplify the design
    - ✓ Minimize the exponential cumulative effect of part quality and quantity.
    - ✓ Conduct thorough DFMEA
    - ✓ Utilize Poka-yoke at design stage also.

- ✓ Document every change thoroughly and completely.
- ✓ Thoroughly design the product "First time right"

Cost of poor quality (COPQ)

- **Supply Chain Cost**
    - ✓ Rework of receipt products
    - ✓ Diagnostics (The cost of investigation, what is wrong)
    - ✓ Re-inspection of rework
    - ✓ Scrap cost
    - ✓ Value of replacement materials and parts
    - ✓ Purchasing actions to procure replacement material.
    - ✓ Analysis of quality problems
    - ✓ Cost of planning and corrective actions costs
    - ✓ Supplier corrective action costs
    - ✓ Scrap/rework generation while set up change to fulfil that defective quantity till first good parts.
    - ✓ Segregation costs
    - ✓ Inventory carrying cost for extra inventory

- **Field Failure Costs**
    - ✓ Dealing with customer complaints
    - ✓ Refund/compensation/Allowance cost
    - ✓ Cost of returned goods
    - ✓ Warranty cost
    - ✓ Recall/retrofit cost
    - ✓ Penalty imposed by customer
    - ✓ Liabilities cost
    - ✓ Goodwill degradation
    - ✓ Damage control costs
    - ✓ Lost sales
    - ✓ Future business threat

- **Appraisal costs**
    - ✓ Incoming inspection cost
    - ✓ In process inspection and testing
    - ✓ Diagnostic cost
    - ✓ Final testing
    - ✓ Internal quality audit
    - ✓ Field quality audit
    - ✓ Corrective actions costs on all above non-conformance
    - ✓ Equipment test and calibration

- **Prevention Costs**
    - ✓ Quality planning
    - ✓ Quality program
    - ✓ Training
    - ✓ Designing in quality and reliability
    - ✓ Process control (SPC)
    - ✓ MSA
    - ✓ FMEA
    - ✓ Quality audits
    - ✓ Supplier development and upgradation
    - ✓ Preventive maintenance

❖ **Energy Cost**

- By shifting the focus of production decisions away from capacity utilization and towards a demand driven models, you can make the decision to scale back production during slow periods without interrupting throughput.
- Even on shop floor, there are many ways to capture energy savings which can have a significant impact on your company's bottom line.
- Preventive maintenance, repairing air and oil leakages, air compressor's air leakages and strategically scheduling

equipment start-up, you can supplement your energy conservation efforts.
- Voltage is directly proportional to current. It means, if voltage will reduce, current consumption will reduce.
- Reduce your voltage supply and save reducing the voltage supply that comes into your business premises from 240 volts to 220 volts, means your equipment will use less energy.

  ➢ **Voltage Optimization**
    o An average savings of 12–18% on electricity bills, even few Indian companies (Manufacturer of voltage optimizer) offers a simple way to save money. They will install the instrument and will establish the saving results too.
    o It reduces maintenance cost as your equipment will be more efficient. It is a common sense, when you will use less energy, it means less wear & tear.
    o Average **ROI** (Return on Investment) of such type of equipment is 2–3 years. It is not bad option at all. Less than 4 years should be acceptable for annual budget clearance.
    o Such types of equipment have minimum life up to 20 years.
    o It has zero side effects on facility.

- An energizer can reduce the running costs of display refrigerators and non-perishable product chiller cabinets by up to 30% a year.
- An energy monitor displays your energy usage as you are using it so you can take actions when you see that consumption is high.

  ➢ **Energy Monitor**
    - Displaying real time energy usage data, an energy monitor is a simple way of seeing how much energy your business is consuming and when it using it,

such information that can help you change your energy usage pattern.

- But how to use it?

  ✓ Set daily energy use targets.
  ✓ See, in real time, what happens when you turn light and appliances on and off.
  ✓ Compare how much energy your business is using from one day to the next day (In 24 hours cycle).
  ✓ This energy monitor comes as part of a complete energy saving kit. It helps to motivate and educate employees of your company.
  ✓ When your employees will start monitoring this data, they will force to take counter measures to reduce the consumptions.
  ✓ You may compare per unit energy consumption with per unit of final products.

➢ **Energy Audit**

  o It carried out by an expert either on-site or over the phone- will help you to see where most of your energy bill is going, how you could save money.
  o One of energy saving consultant will visit your business in person.
  o He/They will assess your current energy consumption by looking at your heating, ventilation, air conditioning, lighting, refrigeration, electrical equipment, water usage and other sources of energy consumption.
  o After the assessment, you will receive an action plan, created specifically for your business. It will be in detail about 8–10 energy saving measures listed in order of potential impact.

- o Next to each measure, you will see how much it's likely to cost you to implement and how much energy you could save as a result helping you to conduct Cost Vs benefits analysis.
- ➤ Use a programmable or smart thermostat to save money on air conditioning.
- ➤ Reduce your climate control and lighting system's work load and carbon footprint by:
  - o Double-pane window: Double-pane windows are better insulator than old school type single-pane window.
  - o Light blocking blinds and curtains: use blackout curtains on south and west facing window.
  - o Tight seals: If you work in an older structure and weather-strip common heat loss points then exterior window and door frame, utility line entries and air vents should be perfectly tight sealed.
- ➤ Solar water heater: It uses the power of sun to heat your fresh water supply.
- ➤ Power down/switched off all non-essential lights, appliances and machinery after hours.
- ➤ Actually it is a painful exercise but straight forward way to reduce your company's electricity bills without affecting its operations.
- ➤ Once you and your team get in the habit of following through, it's painfully easy too.
- ➤ In white collar office, personal computer workstations comprise the single biggest non-essential energy suck, so make sure everyone powers their down before heading out.
- ➤ Shut off overhead and desk lights too.

- ➢ Leave instructions for building cleaning crews or night watchman to do so when they are done.
- ➢ In restaurants and light industrial facilities that don't run over night, power off machinery and appliances not required for safety or storage. In other words, turn off the oven, not the freeze.

❖ **Overhead Costs**

- To monitor and control the expenses associated with running the factory, often referred as overhead costs.
- Building, utility, supply, storage, handling, travel, supervisory & administrative costs, all add to manufacturing costs.
- Set budget for these support costs and review them on a weekly, monthly and yearly basis.
- Research purchase versus rental options for cost saving.
- Limit employee costs to those, which benefits production or increase sales.
- Keep debt and interest expense as low as possible.
- Monitor tooling and supply costs.

❖ **Work Smarter**

- Eliminating monotonous tasks through the use of technology is a great way to optimize your labour costs.
- By automating or consolidating repetitive manual processes, you can increase product quality.
- Improve throughput time and potentially cut down costs.
- Technology is always evolving and offers new ways of making tasks much easier to complete. Touchless productions already started in paint industries in India itself. Now time will come and operations shall be carried out on voice base only. You will tell and those data shall be automatically fed into the system. Self-process planning shall be automatically started and output (without any defects) shall be run consistently.

- **Technology for**
    - Achieving low cycle time
    - Auto clamping and de-clamping
    - Auto tool movement
    - Auto programming
    - Auto machining
    - Auto loading/unloading
    - Auto counting
    - Auto marking
    - Auto inspecting
    - Auto segregating defective parts
    - Auto marking on ok & defective part
    - Auto washing
    - Auto drying
    - Auto packing
    - Auto packaging
    - Energy efficient
    - Statistically (SPC) informative

It can be implemented both on shop floor and offices.

❖ **Sell Scrap to Vendors**

- *One's trash is another man's treasure"*. We do think selling off your scrap to vendors is a useful decision and act but yet often overlooked.
- Approach to cashing in on metal, batteries and electronics that may, otherwise be disposed of.

❖ **Better Negotiations Possibility**

- Building long lasting relationship with suppliers and freight companies is essential to your company's success but that doesn't mean you have to accept the first price presented by them. Take advantage of your position as a manufacturer and try to negotiate a better rate.

Features of Good Plant Layout for Cost Optimization

- Planning of the space available for all the activities and facilities associated with manufacturing with a view to enable the plant to function effectively & efficiently. In other words, people, workstations and equipment should be arranged to optimize flow, minimize waste and boost productivity.
- Plant layout identically involves the allocation of space and the arrangement of equipment in such a manner that overall operating costs are maintained.
- Plant Layout is not only engineering function but its combination of engineering & management function. It's combination of arts & science.
- Efficient space utilization: Efficient space = neither excess nor less space. Land cost and rental are increasing day by day. Excessive use of space means, walking will increase. So the arrangement of machines, service points and workmen movement should be done in such a way that space is properly utilized.
- Easy material handling: Double touching and carrying materials for a certain distance for next processing is cost added activities. It should be eliminated or reduced by provisioning of flat sheet, roller conveyor, chutes, pick n place mechanism (LCA), hoist or lift. If we focus on same workstations height and minimum or no distance between two operations, then it can be completely eliminated.
- Flexibility: Only change is constant. Innovations and upgradations in technology, manufacturing methods & processes are in fast pace in the world. So our layout should be flexible enough to adapt to changes.
- Accessibility: Manufacturing, maintenance, stores, tool room and other servicing facilities should be easily accessible without any hindrance. To achieve this purpose, there must be sufficient space between machines so that raw materials, machines and men are able to move freely from one place to other.

- Less movement: Ideally there should be no leg movement and no excessive arm stretch. If not possible then there should be very minimum (1 step) movement of men and machines. Movement should be direct as far as possible because indirect handling of materials always adds unnecessary cost without any value addition.
- Co-ordination & Integration: A good layout would be able to co-ordinate all operations. The layout should be designed taking into account of the inter-relationship between various equipment, departments and personnel. Complete pictures of the organization's working to be considered at this stage only.
- Visibility: Work should be arranged in such a way that there is no problem in supervision, co-ordination and control. Raw materials, WIP and finished goods should have specific storage points and must be visible at all times. This would reduce the possibility of misuse and theft.
- Reduced discomfort: actual comfortable & needed working environment level such as proper lighting, dustless, fumeless, noiseless, smokeless, vibration less and excessive heat control to be ensured. These are basic needs for working.
- Adherence to statutory regulations: Regulations of factory act should be taken care of on top priority with regards to health, safety and welfare of employees. Adherence to the above regulations would minimize accidents, will reduce absenteeism due to sickness contributing to improved productivity.
- Preservations of materials and equipment: The layout should contain safeguards against fire, moisture, theft and general deterioration of equipment and materials. There should be adequate and safe storage locations. There should be provision for storing inflammable materials separately and in a safe manner.

Some Must Be Facilities for the Plant

- Jogging track inside shop floor (along walls)
- Plantations in plant campus.
- No earth should be visible in entire company area. These should be green lawns, tar road or concrete flooring.
- No trucks, fork lifts inside shop floor.
- Clean, dry and smell free workmen toilet with push system water tap.
- No nails to be used anywhere in the factory premises.
- All employees should wear uniforms, shoes and necessary gadgets.
- Noise free D.G sets and compressors.
- Clean change room and rest room facilities for workmen.
- Good recreational facilities.
- Well-equipped training and meeting room.
- Appropriate firefighting equipment to be placed.
- Steel frame with localised lighting display board (Departmental board and central board).

Some "Do for Undo" Activities ☹ (These Points to be Discouraged Because These Are Ghost Costs)

- Use of air guns for cleaning of components, jigs, fixture and machines to be completely avoided.
- Use of hammer in assembly operation/doing adjustment while part loading on the work stations.
- Direct usage of wires into electrical plugs, without socket while welding, fan connection etc.
- Wet floor due to chips and coolants and floor cleaning by the sweepers in the line. Our motto should be cleaned without cleaning/swept without sweeping.
- Use of wire/clothes to tie electric cables.
- Hand written instructions pasted on the machine or wall or door or window.
- Use of nonstandard stickers.

- Keeping machines directly on floor (Any machines).
- Loose wire and cables on machine and work stations.
- Use of bare hands for applying grease to components/assembly.
- Painting of machines/fixtures done by unskilled persons.
- Use of files/hacksaw blades and knives for deburring.
- Use of metal rod to remove the components from the fixtures.
- Use of tray below the machine to collect leaked oils.
- Termination of the earthling wire is done without proper thimble.
- Unwanted documents are displayed on workstation.
- Operation standards displayed at the work station is difficult to read (either due to language or font sizes or poor photocopies/prints).
- Card board packing/shims are used for work table height/jigs & fixtures adjustment.
- Dipping the components with bare hands in packing/oil both for rust prevention or cooling.
- Material storage and handling like coconut.
- Coolant changing frequency based on time period instead of actual usage.
- Instruments calibration based on time period instead of actual usage.
- Use of wooden/metal platform by operators at work stations.
- Monitoring the machine wise output instead of line output.
- Safety shoes rules not followed by staffs.
- Bins are kept directly on floor.
- Not using designated dust bins to disposed of different types of wastage materials (hazardous, bio degradable, recyclable, reusable)
- Sitting working by the operator on the line/shop floor.

Some "BAD HABITS" to be Discontinued

- Spitting on walls/shop floor corners.
- Not keeping glasses/tea cups at designated place.
- Not using dust bins to throw the waste papers.
- Keep PC on after working hours (Not off).
- Tools are not kept at proper place (Shadow board) after use.
- Identification of non-confirming materials not done immediately.
- Coming late in every meeting.
- Using mobile phone in the shop floor.
- Cross talking/chatting/using mobile phones in the meeting and training programme.
- Keeping metal touching against the wall at undesignated area.
- Use of standard bin colour is not followed.
- Components are kept in/on around the machine.
- Measuring instruments are kept on the machine and not at designated place.
- Violating/bypassing the working systems like Poka-yoke.
- Violating/bypassing the safety systems/procedures such as two hand button switches, safety guards etc.
- Not updating system related documents as DWM (Daily work management) practices.
- Coming late to the factory without information.
- Availing leaves without permission.
- Frequent short leaves.

Wish to Become "GOOD to GREAT" Company?

GOOD is not enough,

    If **BETTER** is possible,

    Try for the **BEST**,

To become **GOOD to GREAT!**

Please assess your plant, are these points implemented/in working culture of your plant? Simply put YES/NO against each point and plan for implementation where you find answer is "NO"!

1. **Policy driven company?** (Quality policy, Environmental policy, Safety policy, Employee's policy, promotional policy, Retention policy, warranty policy, Leave policy, Lease policy, Scrap disposal policy, procurement policy, QMS related policy, BRC certification related policy, Customer expectation related policy, Award/reward policy, CSR related policy, ...)
2. **Glass visual company?** (Nothing hidden/transparent)
3. **5S score** = minimum 85 (Lowest point of any department)?
4. **ITR (Inventory Turnover ratio)** = 30 + ?
5. **VAPCO (Value addition per person of the company)** = minimum 8?
6. **Receipt quality PPM** = less than 100?
7. **KAIZEN minded company?**
8. **TEI (Total employees involvement/engagement in continual improvement)** = 100%?
9. **Outgoing quality PPM** = ZERO?
10. **Breakdown** = less than 500 minutes for 50 working machines/month?
11. **SMED** (Single minute exchange of Dies/moulds) = set up time in single digit? (9 minutes?)
12. **Hammerless company?** (No forced fitment)
13. **Noise less company?** (No loose)
14. **Paperless company?** (Digital)
15. **Supervisor less Company?** (System should be such that no supervision required for production, quality or safety)
16. **Leakage free company?** (No water, oil, air, coolant or information leakages from company)
17. **Accident free company?** (No unsafe actions/No unsafe conditions)

18. **Dustless company?** (Plantation/grass/tar covered/concrete flooring), No visible soil?
19. **Rust less company?** (Nothing exposed in open condition, proper storage provisioning for all)?
20. **Forklift less company?** (Rolling material handling)?
21. **Company like garden**/hospital type cleaned/airport type toilet/Temple type pure?
22. **Rack less company?** (No storage more than 5 feet height even in store)?
23. **Pallet less company?** (Pallet means material is resting, not flowing)
24. **Poly bag less company?** Gunny bag less company?
25. **Scrap on wheel?** (shift wise from shop and weekly disposal from company) (Respect for scrap is needed by providing proper storage)
26. **Dent less company?** (storage like coconut? or Car parking)
27. **Idle time less company?** (No waiting for material, machine, man, approval for start-up)
28. **Red inventory less company?** (Obsolete/suspected/undecided/non-moving/undecided stocks)
29. **Rack height less than 5 feet in store?**
30. **Coconut to car parking like storage in store, floor?**
31. **Nothing on direct floor?** (Sweeping is difficult)
32. **Jogging path along with wall?** Through gangway?
33. **Nothing pasted on wall**/door/window/whiteboard/toilet/training room/reception/entry gate). It should be pinned up!
34. **6 faces machines cleaning in the start of shift?**
35. **Much low cost automation on bottleneck operations?**
36. **Transparent electric panel/almirah?**
37. **Direction of flow/rotations?**
38. **Shadow board culture for tool storage?**

39. **Training kits for maintenance/R&D?**
40. **Spares on wall?** (To maintain essential spares & elimination of searching time)?
41. **First aid boxes in practice?**
42. **Operation number display in product layout?**
43. **Safety calendar on gate?** (But it must be truthfully maintained, not for impressing visitors)
44. **Cellular layout for specific product line?**
45. **Continuous disposal of swarf during machining?**
46. **Direction boards on every turning point?**
47. **Constant pushing water taps even in toilet?**
48. **Doors with door closure/sensors?**
49. **SOP driven company?** (For every process of the company even for HR/Accounts/Marketing)
50. **Standing working like doctor in operation theatre?**
51. **Concept of FUGUAI tree implementation & maintenance by shop floor supervisor & elimination of fuguai leaves by maintenance staff?**
52. **Manager's model machine on floor?** (TPM initiation)
53. **MY MACHINE concept by operators** (TPM on machine)?
54. **Effective & Efficient use of DWM (Daily work management) board?** (Decisions/actions on bottleneck)
55. **HOME DOCTOR concept for machine/process/product/tools?**
56. **Uniform for all and Uniform cleaning policy implemented?**
57. **Colour coding of pipes/machines/project wise dies/moulds/scrap bin/WIP trolley/storage/rework trolley/Hot/extra cold? Water, oil, air, gas?**
58. **Standardization of display for font size/type of font/base/board?**
59. **Suggestion scheme policy for all?** (suggestion collection, review, decision for implementation, award for the best suggestion)

60. **Talent bank & clear cut retention policy?**
61. **Spider man concept for PPC?**
62. **MILK RUN concept** for collecting out sourcing materials?
63. **Supermarket creation for KANBAN board?**
64. **Zebra marking for divider & fire extinguisher?**
65. **2 – Bins for online** material feeding concept?
66. **Two suggestions**/employee/month?
67. **Yellow band for all poka – yoke stations?**
68. **Internal customer concept** (Maker-checker separately)?
69. **OEE measurement**, monitoring & improvement by engineers?
70. **JIT deliver** (Vendor/internal department/customers)?
71. **QCC culture** and have many winning records at national/international level?
72. **Rolling trophy** for the best performing department & best employees?
73. **P-Q Analysis** based inventory management?
74. **Skill matrix for all employees?** (Especially for workmen/engineers)?
75. **Continual training** needs identification. Plan, module, imparting, evaluation, effectiveness check and recognition system?
76. Established culture for **customer satisfaction survey?**
77. Established culture for **employee's satisfaction survey?**
78. Established culture for **supplier's satisfaction survey?**
79. **The best supplier trophy**/supplier cluster program?
80. **FIXED MEET CULTURE:** customer meet/Employees meet/suppliers meet?
81. **TRACKER REPORTS**: Cell performance tracker/dispatch tracker/supplier tracker?
82. Use of Natural lighting during day? **Solar energy?**
83. Best point/worst point/**fixed point photography culture** and improvement?
84. **KAIZEN competition**/mela/gallery/training?

85. **SCORE/STATUS INDICATOR** – Dash board like aeroplane?
86. **FIFO in culture?**
87. **VA/VE?**
88. **NO chips/oil/grease on floor? Dustless floor?**
89. **TOILETS for ALL** (Not designated as staffs toilet or worker's toilets)?
90. **CANTEEN for ALL?**
91. **SAFETY AUDITS** by top management?
92. **Absenteeism less than 3%?**
93. **No inspection to no inspection status** achievement by implementation of multiple poka-yoke?
94. **Continual cost optimisation projects in team for implementation & award?**
95. **Clear out skirts of the plant?**
96. **Talk to: Machine**/process/product finish habit/culture in the plant?
97. **FMEA updating culture** for design/process?
98. **DMAIC for project handling?**
99. **Policy development & updating culture from TOP?**
100. **Strategic sourcing? (Make or buy?)**
101. **AWARDS for: TPM Excellence-Availability, TQM – Capability, TPS – Adequacy?**

Less than 75 marks = No guarantee for survival in coming 5 years

GOOD company = 75 marks

BETTER company = 85 marks

BEST company = 95 marks

GREAT company = 100 + (Adding new benchmark in this list)

Some Cost Saving Ideas for New Start-Up and Small Businesses

- ❖ **Reduce Paper use/Paperless company:**
  - Cutting down paper waste is good for your company's bottom line and the environment.
    - ➤ Print and copy double – sided by default.
    - ➤ Use secure electronic file exchange services such as delivered secured, rather than traditional courier services.
    - ➤ Reduce waste paper for scratch or notes.
    - ➤ Tightened margins and shrink fonts on printed reports.
    - ➤ Inform vendors and other sources of postal mail when employees no longer work for your company.
    - ➤ Take your company's name off from direct mailing lists wherever legally and practically possible.
    - ➤ Replacing your existing printer with one that prints on both sides of paper, thus reducing paper wastes and costs.
    - ➤ Going green is not only a great P R move, it's also a smart financial move.

- ❖ **Encourage Telecommuting**
  - **Align Plan Costs with Usage**
    - ➤ Your company probably pays a lot of essential services—telecommunications, cloud storage, book keeping, perhaps even legal support via monthly or annual plans. At minimum you should review these plans once in a year to determine whether they are adequate for your needs.
    - ➤ If you are paying for capacity, that you don't need or use regularly then you can likely down size to a cheaper plan without hurting your business.
    - ➤ If you are routinely exceeding the limits of a lower capacity plan then you could be paying a lot to run over

those limits. For an example, cellular carriers charge 600/to 750/per gigabytes for data overages. Upsizing to a more generous, higher capacity plan might result in a higher monthly fee, but it could save you hundreds in the long run.

➢ Lookup in the cloud: you can save lot of time and resources by adopting cloud computing. Employees can work remotely and use on line collaboration on tools to get the work done.

➢ Telework compatible job: in other foreign country, nearly 50% workforce holds a telework compatible job and 80% to 90% of workers want to be able to telecommute at least some of the time. But only 20% to 25% telecommute at all.

➢ Telecommuting also directly impacts companies and employees bottom lines by:

- o Reducing utility costs through lower electricity and water usage.
- o Reducing the amount of space required to house employees in a central location (by replacing dedicated cabins and desks with collaborative workstations that home based employees can use when they visit office.
- o Reducing time lost to commuting and travelling.
- o For example, you can use drop box to share files, profit books for managing finances on line and skype to have virtual meetings. We do understand that a first meeting is important and should be done face to face but all follow-up meetings can be done virtually.

❖ Factory/Office Space Cost

- Use space more effectively and efficiently.
- Scientific plant layout which includes required ergonomics, machine cleaning, machine breakdown handling, preventive maintenance, material loading-unloading, space for input and output materials. Dies & tools storage near to machine, swarf disposal and coolant cleaning, all needed required optimum space around the machine. In scientific layout such type of needed are covered.
- Similarly in office area, there is some scientific norm like square feet area required for one person for smooth working.
- Area can be optimised by collaborative workstations
- Mobile device usage station.
- Multipurpose rooms (conference rooms that double as breakrooms) is a great news for rent conscious business owners and executives.

❖ Sensible Healthcare Changes

- Most employees benefits package include some form of healthcare coverage. Salaried employees expect from employers to provide for their health care needs, and it's probably right thing to do anyway. It's needed and it is known to insurance market too.
- Insurance market having different types of plan to attract customers but all leads to premium amount. Different agencies have similar plan but different premium amount. They add some unique and rare category norms to hike the premium amount.
- Look for different plans from different agencies. Prepare one matrix – benefits Vs premium amount and choose the least quotes.
- Some insurance agencies offer a very good discount on numbers of candidates. We can take benefits for that also

❖ **Maintenance Cost**

- Use hi-tech alternatives to legacy systems. We have seen, every old machines are bad in energy consumptions. Without thinking much, old machines which are 15+ year's age should be replaced with new energy efficient machines.
- This action will reduce energy cost and parallel will improve reliability, productivity and safety for the plant.

❖ **Buy Used**

- Nowhere in your company by laws does it say that you must buy only shiny new equipment. So why not buy gently used items when it makes sense to do so.
    - Office technology such as printers and copiers.
    - Personal technology, such as refurbished smart phones, tablets and laptops.
    - Vehicle such as delivery vans and general purpose company cars.
    - Senior positions must be excluded from this policy.
    - Storage equipment such as liquid vats and bins.
    - Assembly and packaging equipment.
    - Used furniture.
    - You can save between 50–70% amount by buying used computer equipment, copiers and office furniture from the classified sites such as OLX or Quikr .
    - In such cases, you can negotiate directly with the seller and get a good deal.
    - If you are not feeling techy, turn up to local newspaper and see the dedicated "classified" page, which are other good sources of used equipment.

❖ **Pay Invoices as Early as Possible**

- It improves brand image.
- Social image updating tools.

- Many vendors offer small but meaningful discounts to clients that pay invoices ahead of scheme.
- It's common for vendors to knock 2% off the invoice total when clients pay in full within 10 days after receipt of materials instead of usual 30 days, 45 days, 60 days, 75 days. 90 days and some are following even for 120 days.
- All these payment brackets must have different discount norms, if not, and then it should be. We should try to encash maximum benefits by paying too early or other extreme.
- We can get benefits at "cash payment" too.
- As long as paying early does not negatively impact your cash flow, it usually makes financial sense to do so.
- It's doubly true in low interest environment, where the cost of short term borrowing to bridge any short fall is unlikely to exceed the value of the discount.

❖ **Make-in-Kind Exchanges (Called as Barter)**

- Think beyond cash, when that cash supply gets low, which is a common thing in case of small business, and then don't close the door on getting what you need.
- Today, most transactions use a currency backed by central banks, but that doesn't mean non-monetary exchange is completely obsolete. There are limits to what and how much you can barter, but it's worth looking into these arrangements if cash is extremely tight or you think your products or services make valuable trade.

❖ **Advertisement Cost**

- Traditional advertising is really very expensive.
- A prime time broadcast at TV's commercial channels, the average cost per 1000 impressions was nearly 1500/ in 2008 that works out to about 15–20 lacs per 30 seconds spot on an average. It is needless to say, most small business can't afford that kind of expenses.

- Paid social media (Facebook, twitter…) advertising is much cheaper.
- In some cases, you don't have to pay for social media advertising at all, if you devote time and manpower to engaging your company's fans and building your social following organically, you can reach thousands of current or perspective customers without spending a pie.
- Traditional advertising methods like buying print or TV advertisements and putting up hording can get very expensive these days.
- Explore new tools like google AdWords & Facebook ads to advertise your products to the targeted audience.
- You can target users from a specific city, age group, income group, profession group, positional title group; industries type group, interest groups and demographics and get good returns on your marketing investment.
- Be a good neighbour: split advertising and promotion costs with neighbouring businesses.
- You can jointly purchase the hording space or take your marketing alliance further by sharing mailing lists, distribution channels and suppliers with businesses that sell complementary goods or services.
- You might have seen the TV advertisements where DTH box comes bundled with a TV. Explore opportunities to promote your products and save on marketing expenses.
- It's important to make sure that the partnership is mutually beneficial for both the parties otherwise it will not yield the desired results.
- Encourage words-of-mouth marketing. It comes in different flavours:
  - ➢ Referral programs that pay existing customers to refer new customers.

- College brand ambassador programs that pay young people to advertise about their employers product on campus.
- Social sharing communities on Pinterest and other digital media, and online review directories.

❖ **Encourage Effective Time Management**

- Time is money which means wasted time is wasted money. Every minute you and your team spend procrastinating is a minute that is not being spent on value added work.
- Procrastination can be as innocuous as stopping by a coworker's desk for a brief, non-work related chat, or as problematic as ducking out of the office for hours at a time to run personal errands.
- If chronic procrastination is a problem at your office, figure out why it is happening and take appropriate action to address it.
- Procrastination is not a catch all culprits for office productivity woes. Some people are better at time management than others. Before singling out easily distracted or apparently inefficient employees for coaching or discipline, implement scalable systems that holds everyone accountable, such as time tracking requirements and benchmark time frames for standardized task completion.

❖ **Use Contract Labour for Non-Core Work**

- Freelancers and independent contractors are easier to hire and cheaper to keep employed than traditional employees, provided you have an enforceable freelance contact to set expectations and mitigate risk on both sides of the relationship.
- You are not expected to provide freelancers with health insurance benefits, pre-tax retirement accounts, family leave or paid time off. You just need to pay them for completed work.

- It's important not to over rely on freelancers and contractors as they are likely to be less loyal and may have other relationship that distract from their work for your company. But for one-off project and ongoing, non-core activities, they can serve as the secret sauce that keeps your company's labour cost under control.

❖ **Invest in Your Employees and Long Term Contractors**

- It costs more than you think to hire an employee, especially one with in-demand skills or specialized knowledge.
- one survey discloses that replacing a typical employee costs about 20% of the employee's salary.
- Retain talented employees, even if it requires you to spend a bit more on salaries and benefits. If it keeps a high potential worker in the fold for an extra year, it will return back 20% additional.

❖ **Wise Capital Investments**

- You have to spend money to make money.
- Every dollar that you invest in your business has a rate of return. But it can sometimes take years for return to materialize.
- If your credit is good enough, you can use a small business credit card to reward responsible spending on inventory and equipment you would purchase anyway.
- The best business credit cards reliably return 1.5% to 2% on spending, either on the form of cash back or miles that can be used towards free travel.
- In some cases, the rate of return is even better, as long as you pay your balance in full each month and only use your card for purchases that you have anyway, you will come out ahead.
- Keep in mind that some cash back credit cards and travel credit cards carry annual fees but you can offset those with moderate to heavy use.
- Using a business credit card, builds credit, which comes in handy if you need larger loans or lines of credit down the road?

Sanju: The Latest Blockbuster

A film based on biography, how a good family produces bad products, how working environment changes the product life cycle from the "BEST to WORST." Discipline is the first criteria for good product quality otherwise every resource will add only cost, not value. Absence of SOPs (either for better product quality or for better human life) will affect always adversely Good machine can also produce bad products, if working environment is not good.

You will reach in the darkest era, if the goal of all employees will be not same as goal of the company. In this film, the best father & the best mother have their own goal and their kids have entirely different goal of life. Final results are now known to all.

The Best machines + The Best raw material + Absence of SOPs + bad environment (lack of process control) = Bad product and finally customers dissatisfaction. Such products, even after 3 times rectifications/rework will not fulfil the end customer's expectations. Segregation and re-heat treatment will be additional cost, not value addition. Those products cannot be used as designed or expected but only can be used as a kid's toy (Munna Bhai MBBS).

So, for the best quality, robust SOPs+ Good working environment + 5S discipline are mandatory!

❖ **Treasury Management**
- Money saved is money earned.
- This may sounds a big word for any new start-up or very small business owner but it's one of effective way of generating money on idle funds. Current accounts with bank,does not give any interest on idle funds in account, one can invest via mutual funds in debt funds for duration as low as 2 days and look forward for tentative interest of 8% pa. There is online investment facility now a day with zero paper work. Any small amount generated can take care of your phone bill or electricity bill.

❖ **Restructure Your Loans**

- If you have taken a loan and it's instalments are causing a burden on your monthly cash flow, just talk to your bank. Most banks can give an option to either pause it for a specific period or help you restructure to increase the tenure and reduce the instalment. Alternatively, you can talk to other banks for lower interest rates and improve your cash flow.
- Debt is generally your enemy. Before embracing small business financing options that put you in hock to big banks or venture capitalists, tap your personal finances and friends-and-family networks for interest free start-up capital. Every dollar of interest that you pay is a dollar that won't accrue to bottom line.

❖ **Decrease Your Locational Costs**

- The best way to reduce high location costs is to relocate a lower-cost region, but that is not always practical or even possible, especially if you are an independent professional with deep family roots in your current backyard.
- If moving is not an option, you need to understand your location costs, identify acceptable ranges for each major line item, and learn how to tweak the numbers in your favour.
- Commercial rent: if your business occupies a space of its own, you have to pay rent on it. To save money in rising rental market, try negotiating a lower rental rate on a long term lease.

❖ **Everything Is Negotiable**

- Unless it's clearly spelt out in a binding contract, every listed price is negotiable.
- Bulk discount/high volume discount
- Locational discount for higher off take.
- Discount or bonuses for new client referrals.

❖ Pool Purchasing Power

- Now a day, homebuyers have come together and manage to get a good deal from the builder. Find other small business owners and collaborate with them to save money on supplies and other goods.
- Always ask for a discount: They may not advertise it, but many top retailers will discount their items for small business owners. You just have to take the initiative to ask.
- Sometimes, you can even get discounts when you pay within the credit period. All you have to do is to ask.

❖ Evaluate Employees Perks and Fringe Benefits on the Merits

- In many industries, especially in software, competition for talent is fierce. On top of juicy, equity packages and generous time-off allowance, many tech employers offer fabulous perks and fringe benefits in a constant arms race to attract ultra-qualified engineers and designers.
- Free catered lunch every day is more practical. Employees have to eat after all.
- However overtime. They can affect profitability. If you are locked in a fierce battle to attract and retain talent, it is better to offer higher starting pay, juicier performance bonuses, and better benefits packages (particularly healthcare and retirement accounts).
- To boost morale, substitute expensive perks to cheaper and social ones. Example, swap the wet bar in your office kitchen for a weekly happy hour where employees pay their one way, and ditch the company-wide theatre outings for optional excursion to free.

❖ Hire Smart and Inexperienced People

- Experience is a true asset for any organization. It cannot be bought within a day but it is not everything, and it comes at a

cost. More and more technological sound companies now hire fresh college graduates and then train them for a month or two. It turns out to be very cost effective than hiring an experienced person.
- For critical work scenario, you have no option but to go for experienced people but in most cases, strategy of training fresher's works.

❖ **Limit Travel Expenses**

- Every business is different. For an example, you can't limit travel expenses if your duties don't require you to travel, and you can't downsize your office space if you are working out of a home office.
- For larger meetings, virtual meeting systems with telepresence capabilities can easily replace office powwow and they are not as expensive too.
- Limiting company-paid travel is an even better deal for your business. sure, there is no substitute for team building at industry conventions, professional meetups, or annual parties. But that doesn't mean you need to travel for every client meeting or satellite office check-in.

Still, it is virtually certain that your business ledgers contain at least some financial fat to trim, even if you think that you have plucked all the low hanging fruit, it may be worth to take another look. It won't cost you anything and it could produce a significant payoff in time.

❖ **Review All Expenses (Even the Smallest One)**

- If you can't monitor, you can't improve.
- You can't manage something which you don't track. So, if you are not keeping records of all your expenses then you should start doing it right now.
- A good accounting software can help you to categorise and compile all expenses and help you to take measure to reduce them.

- I know one example from my first company that used to order pizzas every Friday for the team. When their accountant told them that the annual bill ran into lakhs, owner was in a rude shock.

❖ **Unnecessary Expenses Must Be Tracked & Killed**

- It is recommended that you should review your budget with a magnifying glass and making sure that all of your expenses are still necessary. Example-perhaps you purchased a magazine subscription a long time ago that you no one reads. Check all such expenses and get rid of unnecessary ones.

❖ **Use Open Source Software**

- You can save substantial amount of money, if you start using open source software. When you are going to order new laptops for your team, you can go for the ones without widow O s. These are cheaper and can run open source O s.

❖ **Reduce Numbers of Land Lines Phones**

- If you are one of those businessman that still using landlines, it's time to think again. There was a time when landline phone was a necessity but it is no longer the case. Mobile phones are cheaper and offer much flexibility. You can use cloud telephony system to route calls between mobile numbers.

❖ **Be Aggressive with Past-Due Accounts**

- Make a list of customers whose payment has past the due date. Start calling them and follow up for the payment. Get aggressive and express your urgency with them. If you do it right, some customers might release the payment on the same day.

❖ **Online Selling**

- By now, you probably know that online commerce is a big deal. Earlier, it used to take a lot to build your own e-commerce store.

But now a day, it is easy to set up seller accounts on e-commerce market places such as Flipkart, snap deal, or eBay. Sites like Amazon even offer their warehouse to store your inventory. This can save huge costs in marketing and inventory maintenance. In fact, this is something which you can let you operate from a small room.

❖ Be Reluctant to Give Credit

- If you do extend credit, thoroughly check the client's credit background and offer credit only, if they have a good repayment history. Most of the times we take emotional decisions but for less than credit worthy accounts its advised to consider the following options:
    - ➢ Collect some partial payment in advance.
    - ➢ Send partial shipment.
    - ➢ Request letters of credit.
    - ➢ Ask for personal guarantee
    - ➢ A pledge of assets.

Apart from all this, just try to be reluctant and delay your decisions to offer credits.

❖ 3 Bids for Every Sales and Purchase

- I have personally experienced this need at one organization during disposal of unwanted stocks/machines/& other items. This scrap dealer was associated with that company since last more than 16 years. I had joined very recently so focused on disposal actions for few items.
- After few weeks, I called for 3 quotations from different sources and fortunately his quote was at maximum.
- If you use services like just dial, you will get calls from at least 3–4 vendors, who will be ready to negotiate with you.

- **Stay on Top of Your Taxes**
  - Close to year end, schedule a tax planning meeting with your accountant to shift income and expenses. For example, shift receivable income into the next year to decrease this year's taxes. Your accountant will be the best person to advice you.
  - Again using good accounting software from the start of your business, can save you lot of time and energy during year-end tax preparation.

- **Join an Association**
  - Many trade and business associations have reasonable membership fees and offer discounts on everything from insurance, travel and car rental to long distance phone service prescriptions and even golf course fees.

- **Run from the Law**
  - Avoiding law suits is a big factor in business success. Try to work out any problems before they grow.

- **Be a Legal Eagle**
  - When hiring an advocate, make sure you have a written fee agreement to prevent surprises. It should include an estimate of the time to be spent on your case and specify what's all the things covered in the fee-including typing or copying and what is not.

- **Query Your Consultants**
  - The professional, you work with regularly, are often easy to bargain with. Thanks to the rapport you have developed with them. Ask your insurance agent, accountant or advocate, how you can cut back on their costs. You would be surprised at the suggestions they might offer on ways to cut your premiums, reduce billable hours or avoid huge retainers.

❖ **Bank on an Early Deposit**

- Make bank deposits early enough in the day, so you get credit (and start earning interest) that day.

❖ **Avoid Cash Advances**

- Credit Card Company usually charge on upfront fee of up to 2% of the advance, with interest accruing immediately.

❖ **Take it with You**

- If you are near to your suppliers then pick up your order yourself or perhaps have a friend or family member can do it for you.

❖ **Make Credit Comparisons**

- If you tend to run unpaid balances on your credit cards at the end of the month, shop for a card with a low interest rate.

❖ **Don't Overlook Crucial Tax Deductions**

- In addition to to being able to deduct a portion of your rent on or mortgage interest and utilities as a business expense, you can also deduct a percentage of various home maintenance expenses, along with a portion of the cost of services such as house cleaning and lawn care.

❖ **Sharing of Expenses**

- If much of your business is conducted at restaurant or you find yourself driving to client's offices, make sure you take those deductions on sharing basis. If you entertain clients or potential clients to discuss current or future project, you can deduct a portion of your entertainment costs. To qualify for this deduction, you must maintain a log of entertainment related expenses you plan to deduct.

- ❖ **Hire Your Family**
  - If your children are at least 18 years old and pay their own taxes, it pays to take advantage of their lower tax bracket. You can essentially transfer income from your business to them to save money.

- ❖ **Mind Some Petty Pointers**
  - Don't get careless about your petty cash account. Though you don't need receipt for expenses under, say 100/, you should still track these expenses.

- ❖ **Shop Around for an Overnight Courier**
  - Overnight delivery rates for the major couriers are competitive. If you are willing to wait few hours or even an extra day you could save.

- ❖ **Be an Early Bird**
  - Send mail early in the day, and you can usually expect to get one-to-two days delivery for the price of a first class stamp.

- ❖ **Avail Bar Code Discounts During Shipping Expenses.**

- ❖ **Commission Your Sales Force**
  - Overheads, salaries, incentives, training costs, fringe benefits and expenses add up when you are hiring your own sales representatives. Contracting independent manufacturer's sales
  - representative, paid on commissions only, is less expensive and often equally effective.

- ❖ **Go with the Flow**
  - Rather than paying for employees who sits idle when business is slow, consider hiring temporary employees to handle surges in business.

❖ **Raise Your Deductible**

- Raising the deductible on your insurance usually lowers your premium.

❖ **Check up on Your Medical Insurance**

- Before choosing a medical insurance career, ask for information on past claims and the loss ratio paid claims to premium.

❖ **Make a Foul Weather Friend**

- *By arranging for an alternative place to run your business, in case if a major disaster, you may be able to save on business interruption insurance, advises the insurance information institute.*

❖ Save on postage by delivering invoices and statements via email.

❖ Download free online forms.

❖ Offer catalogues and broachers as pelf downloads to cut printing and stripping costs.

❖ Turn down the heat or turn up the AC.

❖ Set your printers to draft mode to save ink cost.

❖ Re-fill your own 'printer cartridge.'

❖ Switch your land line telephone on cable.

❖ Check every invoice and verify charges before paying to party.

❖ Review your cellular plan usage and compare rates elsewhere before renewing.

❖ Don't cut marketing, but target your niche to get the most for your ad bucks.

❖ Cross train your employees to help each other during crunch time instead of hiring temporary employees.

- Concentrate on customer service to keep merchandise return rate down.
- Double check addresses before shipping to avoid costly mistakes.
- Include promotional materials in outgoing packages, coupons, newsletters and fliers.
- Use e-mails and social media instead of direct mail to test new offers and coupons for your customers.
- Shop around for better rates on printing, shipping and office supplies items.
- Use free shipping materials from USPS, UPS and FedEx.
- Signup for free business directory listing on line.
- Reuse—Reduce—Recycle
- Share your specialisation in public appearances blogs and social media and get free exposure.
- Join a networking group and find a mentor with more experience to advice you.
- Look for online tools that offer a free basic service (skype) with paid upgrades when you need them.
- Look for rebates/incentives to replace old equipment with newer, more energy efficient system,
- When travelling, use free airport shuttles and eat lunch where there is free Wi-Fi but be sure to follow these Wi-Fi safety precautions.
- Don't book at a conventional hotel without comparing rates with AAA, AARP or credit card discounts.
- Meet clients between meals in a quiet upscale hotel lobby.

- Use free teleconference services.
- When in doubt, go without.
- Manage your own website.
- Daily inventory on key items.
- Switch the facility cleaning from a contractor to underutilized employees.
- Buy used software.
- Insulate where lacking and stuff the cracks to reduce heating and air conditioning bills.
- Opt for shorter work week.
- Publish employee productivity secrets.

Cost Saving Tips

Always start with thorough and realistic reviews:

- Begin with a complete assessment.
- Prioritizing return on investment
- First seek improvement from within

Your factory staff can be a great source of ideas for improving processes. Many times consultants will talk with workers on the shop floor to discuss ideas regarding process improvement, which is right thing also. Because workers on the shop floor are the ones, who consistently using the processes, they have valuable insights into how things can be simplified or improved to generate value.

- **Rewarding employees** with a percentage of cost savings from their improvement ideas, is a great way to fuel their willingness to search for additional ways to save.

- **Reconsider old ideas**, cost saving ideas get sidelined by more pertinent priorities all the time, but that doesn't mean those original ideas were bad ideas.
- By going back and looking at previous proposed cost saving ideas, it's likely you will find one or more great ideas that make sense to implement now or in the near future.
- **QMS system implementation:** Any manufacturing organization focused on consistently providing quality products, improving customer satisfaction and improving processes system.

Food for Thoughts

1. Biased and Weak Consultant!

Consultants and Advisors both are two words in dictionary and have different roles too. We do agree that consultancy is not a charity, but due to only getting service charges for longer term from that organisation, consultant should not be biased. A good consultant means:

1. Act like mentor.
2. Act on facts (data based).
3. Who can help for goal setting?
4. Inputs on fair and clear gaps in resources.
5. Unbiased feedback on resource quality.
6. Should not involve in hiring and purchase.
7. Should not involve in company's internal politics.
8. Should not SUPPORT ONLY TOP management by neglecting other employees.
9. Should be determined with real and necessary needs which should be filled up by Top management to achieve the goal.
10. Should not mix as a family because after mixing, consultant will be biased.
11. Should be firm and fearless (should not negotiate with wrong judgement due to getting service charges only).
12. Tangible target, Standardised operating procedures, Visual improvement and controls.
13. Non-negotiable with repetitive failure and negligence of management.
14. Needed things must be completed on time.
15. If some suggestions are being ignored by management then those must be clarified on top priority.
16. Punctual, disciplined & consistent.

2. Committed Management!

Yesterday was my scheduled visit to one plant 60 km away from my house. I started early and reached at committed time. After closing meeting at 5.30 pm, I felt highly satisfied due to following reasons:-

1. Managing Director and Coordinator were present in the factory on time.
2. Last week's homework completion ranging from 16 to 80%.
3. They have sold 6 trucks (fully loaded) unwanted stocks/materials.
4. Took decision to dispose 4 obsolete machines (out of order/old machines).
5. Many metallic trolleys have been taken out for dismantling and disposal.
6. Six Moulding machines are still in stoppage condition to liquidate excess and unbalanced inventory.
7. Paint procurement stopped for 2 months (except for 1 or 2 most wanted but less stock paints).
8. Pull system started and finished goods vehicles rotation increased by 4 times.
9. Packing materials, sticker's procurement also stopped for 1 month.
10. Electric wiring, localised covers on rotating spindles— works were taken as decided during last visit.
11. They have Spent 30k on leakages arresting projects.
12. Few metallic almirah, cup-boards rectified to make visible from outside.
13. 22 old and obsolete electric motors also disposed of along with one old motorcycle and 4 metallic gates,
14. Unwanted moulds kept separately for disposal.
15. Shadow board concept introduced for tool room.
16. Daily work management (DWM) boards introduced as agreed and implemented. Use of that board was visible to me.
17. 1S/2S started in office filing too.
18. DE flashing contractor replaced with high efficient and systematic contractor who understands single piece flow mechanism.
19. Productivity improved by 16% in one month without any extra actions except layout change and correct 1S/2S.

20. All team members were very happy at the end of the day and greeted me very happily. They assured me to achieve 100% homework completion on time and every time.
21. Spares on wall – started at maintenance department.

When I was about to leave from there, MD came out from his cabin to see off me in very smiling and happy mood. After 5 minutes of my departure, he sent me "Thank You Sir" short messages from his mobile phone.

Yesterday was really great day for me too. I am trying to give 200% to them.

3. Fear for Survival!!

I had received such types of messages from many LinkedIn members:

Dear Sir,

I have not got any job since last 8 months. I am continuously trying by applying every opportunity seen at LinkedIn.

I am not getting any calls for interview, I have contacted many seniors for reference but nothing happened. My last working day in current organisation is 30th April"

Such types of message and calls I am getting from many known connections.

Fear for survival is at sight.

Sir, kindly think, how will my family survive, when salary will stop.

During interview, the toughest question will be—"Are you still working there?" What suitable answers to be given?

If I will not get job in coming 3–4 months then how my house expenses shall be managed?

Should I ask financial help from my relatives?

Or should I try with my near & dear friends at this stage?

Loan against property or personal loan also not be cleared, in case of jobless candidate.

I have already withdrawn my provident funds last year during my sister marriage"

Many unanswered questions…many doubts…dark future…! What to do?

Don't worry my friends! God is for all of us. God has given stomach with two hands and one head. Stay on truth; get updated on new tools, techniques and the best practices in your field. If you are determined to do another job then you will definitely get that.

ये वक़्त भी बदल जाएगा। जब अच्छा वक़्त ज़्यादा दिन नहीं रहा तो ये बुरा वक़्त भी ज़्यादा दिन नहीं रहेगा!!

Last key of your bunch can open your closed fate lock. Keep trying!

4. कोशिश करने वालों की हार नहीं होती!

Anita Tiwari ji is the best friend of my wife was on the way to "MAA VAISHNODEVI YATRA" and returned back on Saturday evening to Faridabad. She visited my house yesterday at 11.30 am for Prasad distribution. She asked my wife: भाई साहेब ख़ुश नहीं दिख रहे हैं, कुछ हुआ है क्या?" My wife told her about my ankle twisting and manuscript deleting episode to her. She expressed deep concerns and started motivating me.

कुमार साहेब, जो कुछ होता है वो सब अच्छे के लिए होता है। तिवारी साहेब और मैं, जब माता रानी के दरबार के लिए चले, तो बार बार तिवारी साहेब बोलते थे कि मेरी तबियत ख़राब हो गयी, मुझे अब आगे बढ़ा नहीं जा रहा। दूसरे जो इनकी कम्पनी के दोस्त थे वो अपनी पत्नी के साथ तेज़ी से चलते हुए हमलोग से काफ़ी आगे निकल गए। हमलोग धीरे धीरे चलते रहे। अर्ध कुमारी मोड़ पर वो रुक कर

चाय पानी पीते हुए हमदोनो को देख कर बोले कि आप लोग आगे बढ़ो क्योंकि मेरी गति आपलोगों से दुगुनी है। जितनी देर में आप लोग एक बार जाएँगे उतनी देर में हमलोग 3 बार दर्शन कर आएँगे। वो ख़ुशफ़श्मी में बैठे रहे और हमलोग धीरे धीरे चलते रहे! जब हमलोग दर्शन करके खाना खा रहे थे तब ये दोनो खच्चर पर चढ़े ऊपर आए और तब तक इतनी देर हो गयी कि बोले अब साहस नहीं है बस यहीं से जल अर्पण कर देता हूँ! अंत में हमदोनो ही जीत गए जो रुके थे वो हार गए। रुकें नहीं, यात्रा जारी रखें!

आपको सफलता मिलेगी!फिर से।

5. Leaders with Guts and Passion

Industries need LEADERS who have

GUTS and PASSION to:

1. Implement his knowledge on floor, not only teaching and preaching in office room.
2. Believe in simple but accurate reporting.
3. Has excellent GEMBA eyes and hands on experience in providing robust solutions.
4. Can help in preparing KPI (Key Performance Indicators) for all departments.
5. Can assist in preparing and reviewing KRA for all employees (Gate to Top chair).
6. Firm believer in actual implementation of IATF QMS/IMS in working systems, not only certification only.
7. Capable technical skills to help in FMEA.
8. Who can take all team members including seasoned old employees with him?
9. Should have courage to tell and convince management for replacement of man, machine and technology in favour of company's goal.
10. Can demonstrate PDCA in his every activity.

11. Must be unbiased with position, designation, locality, castes and religion.
12. Having practical approach for planning implementation and ensuring pro-activeness.
13. Safe and pleasant working environment should be his top priority.
14. Manpower reduction should be last agenda in cost reduction.
15. Can implement TPM on one machine and Lean mfg in one product line.
16. Has good exposure in horizontal deployment tactics.
17. COPQ is not for only presentation but for Zero defect.

6. Leadership Skills

वह पथ क्या ......पथिक कुशलता क्या?
जिस पथ में बिखरें ......,,,,शूल ना हो,
उस नाविक की धैर्य...... कुशलता क्या,
जब धाराएँ ....प्रतिकूल ना हो??

Big goal has always big challenges. Hut can be made in days, but palace required years to complete. Easy path generally guides to bad destination. Every famous temple you will find at mountain surrounded with dense forest. Bar is always at highway or easy to search place.

Similarly true leaders always think differently and unique goal post. They lead from front and strengthen/support from back. Leader's life and behaviour are very simple, helping nature.

A good leader always accepts bigger challenges when systems are not in a good shape. They have capability to rewrite history of SOPs.

I have seen much top management in my short career and also seen that they know:

Productivity is less due to bad machine, wrong SOP, even due to wrong supervisory control but they have fear for change.

Once you find, it's wrong then kindly don't go ahead with the same. Change something before another step!!

7. Manufacturing System Mantra

1. DIS-COVER for DISCOVER
2. GANGA FLOW on machining
3. COCONUT to CAR PARKING
4. NO INSPECTION (Absence of inspection) to NO INSPECTION (Not required inspection)
5. SCRAP on WHEEL
6. CLEANED without CLEANING
7. SEEING is BELIEVING
8. PROACTIVE is PROFIT
9. BURR MANAGEMENT
10. CHIPS MANAGEMENT
11. DE-SKILLED OPERATIONS
12. WISH LESS LUBRICATION
13. KAIZEN is a CULTURE
14. 5S is a HABIT
15. PDCA is the YOGA
16. TRAINING is the INVESTMENT
17. LEAKAGE has no HOLIDAYS
18. LOOSE is LOSS
19. OPERATOR is BOSS
20. DWM is mfg DHRMA
21. CLEANING is INSPECTION
22. DOING is IMPORTANT
23. PREVENTION is better than REACTION
24. UNCOVER, DISCOVER, RECOVER
25. QUALITY is an INTENTION

Apply these honestly with PDCA approach, am sure balance sheet will change.

8. Black Friday

My Black Saturday!!

Month's efforts spoiled in seconds. Now I am 50 years old, had chosen to pen down my 24 years of industries learnings in the form of books. For this, took break from my regular working career 2 years back and published two books (PRE-FIT for PROFIT; FIX "n" FINISH) so far. I was penning down manuscript of my 3rd book (COST OPTIMISATION: A Way to convert EXPENSE into ASSET). MS Words file completed for 230 pages and since last few days I was refining it with some more practical insights.

Yesterday morning when I had gone for morning walk with my pet (OREO) then got my ankle twisted. Swelled and unable to walk freely.

I returned back, got bath, prayed and taken breakfast. Breakfast was also not in good taste.

I opened my laptop to give final shape of manuscript because I had committed to publisher to send word file yesterday only.

I was thinking and modifying but by mistake my whole manuscript got deleted in a fraction of seconds.

My all happiness turned into sorrow now. Since last day morning, I am not in good shape of my mind. My 7–8 months efforts vanished in 1 second.

I was determined to devote my full time either in my consultancy or will return back to main working stream as an employee but…! Hard luck. Bad luck !

Now I am in a fix. Should I stop writing?

9. Sleeping Money... Slipping Money!!

Optimisation of Conveyor Speed is the prime mover of PROFIT WHEEL of any PAINTING Business company? Optimisation will depend upon the desired quality of components. Higher speed means lower coating thickness, dull finish with lower drying time and lower speed will yield higher coating thickness with higher drying time. Higher coating thickness is certainly not a guaranteed result of higher preservation life. Generally thick layer gives lower presentation and high consumption of paints.

It is being noticed that the painting department supervisor or skilled senior operators generally play with this speed. When senior person will be on plant visit, the conveyor speed will be at higher mode and after that it is being reset at lower speed . It means we generally neither get good quality nor cost saving.

Conveyor speeds setting to be in lock under custody of senior supervisor only and always run at REQUIRED SPEED, NOT AT DESIRED SPEED.

Secondly, it is being noticed that only 50% conveyor fixtures are loaded, 50% are running in air only

Finally such company gets only 30% efficiency from that setup which directly affects customer satisfaction and profitability!

Empty moving of conveyor is cost addition, make it fully value addition

10. Too Late but Big Surprise!

There was one small plant in this flower pot. After season, plant naturally died. I taken out all soils from it and after mixing some compost, prepared for planting some other flower or so but due to some reason I have not contacted street gardener since long.

To make it live, I was watering continuously since last 2 months. My wife always put one question—when there is no plant then why are you wasting your time and efforts for watering. Put more water in some other flower pot in which already some plants are there.

Without answering her question, during watering all other flower pots, I continued to water it too. After 2 months, I have seen something green is coming up. When gardener visited last week, I told him, kindly put some good summer flower in it.

He told—sir, ye to Bahut badhiya Plant ismei laga hai, aap dusra kyon lagwana chahte hain?" It's very sweet fruit plant, keep watering in summer too."

HARD and CONSISTENT efforts give SWEET FRUITS always!!

11. You are Not a Businessman!

1. If you don't notice security guard at gate is not fully attentive then you are not a businessman.
2. If you don't notice long queue near worker toilets, then you are not a businessman.
3. If you don't notice fire extinguishers are kept at wrong place then you are not a businessman.
4. If you don't notice grass or flower trimming at plant's garden then you are not a businessman.
5. If you don't recognise the ghost employees then you are not a businessman
6. If you don't notice hard working, punctual and honest employees then you are not a businessman.
7. If you don't notice huge inventory pile up between two operations then you are not a businessman.
8. If you don't notice abnormal noise from machines then you are not a businessman

9. If you don't notice multiple scrap yards in the plant then you are not a businessman
10. If you don't notice leakages in the Plant then you are not a businessman
11. If you don't feel humid and hot working environment inside heat treatments shop then you are not a businessman
12. If you don't notice late coming staffs who stays late in the evening then you are not a businessman
13. If you don't notice loose wiring, slippery floor, dirty toilets, impure water supply and bad food service in the canteen then, you are not a businessman.

12. "5S" Is For Our Family First!!

NEEDED ITEMS/AREAS are required CLEANING!

CLEANING is required for INSPECTION!

INSPECTION is required for DETECTION!

DETECTION is required for CORRECTION!

CORRECTION is required for PREVENTION!

PREVENTION is required for ASSURANCE!

ASSURANCE is required for STANDARDIZATION!

STANDARDIZATION is required for PROFIT!

PROFIT is required for SUSTENANCE & GROWTH!

SUSTENANCE & GROWTH are required for MOTIVATION & BRANDING!

MOTIVATION & GREAT BRANDING are required for CELEBRATION!

CELEBRATION is required for new motivated GENERATION!! and NEW MOTIVATED GENERATION is required for our proud NATION!

OUR NATIONAL MISSION—SWACHH BHARAT, SWASTH BHARAT!

SO,

Create ENVIRONMENT for SUSTENANCE!

GOOD ENVIRONMENT can be created through CULTURE!

CULTURE is nothing but repetition of COLLECTIVE HABIT!

HABIT can be established, if we have DESIRE!

BIRTH of DESIRE comes from our FAMILY!

WE are here for our FAMILY & our family is for US!!

SO,

DO "5S" for your FAMILY!!!

13. Act is Fact!

If you are only DREAMING, if you are only WILLING, if you are only WISHING, if you are only PLANNING, if you are only ORGANISING, if you are only PROVIDING,

BUT if you are not DELEGATING , if you are not ACTING, if you are not REVIEWING, if you are not DECIDING on TIME, if you are not FIXING time bound TARGET, if you are not giving RESPONSIBILITY with certain AUTHORITY, if you are not SUPPORTING with financial BUDGET,

THEN you may be anything but, you are not a REAL BUSINESSMAN, you are not a CEO/COO, you are not VP or PLANT HEAD!!

DREAMING is important, but ACTING is more important!!

MAKING a PROFIT at the cost of employees DEMOTIVATION, Making a PROFIT at the cost of CUSTOMERS DIS-SATISFACTION, Making a PROFIT at the cost of ENVIRONMENT ABUSES

Is not a BUSINESS!!

BE good Business man, be good Leader for getting our country AHEAD in the progressive path!!

Wishing a great success and respect for all BUSINESS MAN!! Be healthy & make our nation healthier!!

14. Benefits By Red Tag Items Disposal:

Some Tangible benefits gained by one automotive plastic mfg company after completion of my 4th visit in one month:

1. WIP 25289 kg reduced to 3260 kg. (Savings—22 lacs).
2. Injection moulding plant (6 machines)—production stopped since last 21 days.
3. Nos of trolleys (6'x3')—131 Nos reduced to 36 Nos.
4. Re-lay outing of final inspection & packing saved 320 square feet area.
5. Working height of all operations at same height.
6. Rearrangement of sticker's almirah & made transparent saved 3 months inventory of that items.
7. Milk – run concept started.
8. Coconut to car parking storage for finished items/corrugated boxes.
9. Disposal of unwanted materials worth of nearly 12 lacs.
10. Paints inventory (Currently 1 month plus) reduced to weekly. Expected saving 15 lacs per month.
11. Multi-locational storage to single location with FIFO concept.
12. Minimum-maximum – Re-order level fixed based on past 1 year consumption pattern.

Rework area reduced to 25%.

15. Needs Of De-Skilling!

There are 3 types of processes: Normal process, Experimental process and special process !

NORMAL PROCESS: Having established SOPs, check points, control points, Work instructions, one point lessons, Established Cp & Cpk, no much changes required during process.

EXPERIMENTAL PROCESSES: Required good technical and analytical skills, no established SOPs, No control and check points, No SPC

After getting desired results all specifications are set.

SPECIAL PROCESSES: Established SOPs, sometimes numerically controlled processes, experience required for setting and corrections, results deviates with minor changes in Time, Temperature, Pressure and compositions, required special skills for decisions to get desired results.

During summer time, such special skilled persons generally take leave to show their importance or they absent on the most needed day/time, generally comes late, feel differently and don't involve in TEAM, never happy with annual increments.

Due to this reasons, discipline of the plant is not maintained at desired level. They play with productivity, quality and cost.

De-killing of such operations are mandatory. Special processes are generally—◆/Heat treatment, painting, printing, Die setting!

TRAIN Now !

16. Good = Lost & Bad = Won?

ये कैसे?

For some team—Aah Sunday, for some team—Waah Sunday!

Every teams were working hard even on last day of this financial year. Till 12 midnight, SAP were running like bullet train, Just after, 12 pm, bosses called their plant heads—CONGRATS!…WELL DONE!! YOUR TEAM DESERVES A BIG PARTY! In the other side, every phone was in vibration mode…no sound at all! Actually this result was not all of a sudden but well known to TOP management too. The difference in both teams were—One team was working on BAD (Breakdown, Accident & Defects) whole year systematically and that team finally WON… HIT the set TARGET with good margin but another team was working on GOOD (G=Generate O=Over production, O = Over processing, & D = Dispatch any quantity/any time/any quality/at any cost to customers) & finally lost the customer's attention. Low or no order and missed the set target.

In this case, BAD = WON ! GOOD = LOST!!

What will be our plan for this financial year?

Only Customer-centric & Robustness in processes will win. Dear friend! Kindly re-assure & re-look at all SOPs (for every product, every processes & every system) in totality. TOTAL is very powerful word in system (TQM, TPM).

17. Head – Aoms (Ayurveda of Manufacturing System)

SCOPE OF WORKING: Dustbin—To—Scrap yard

PERFORMANCE PARAMETERS:

- Delighted Customers,
- Motivated & Happy employees family,
- Fully satisfied Top management &
- Stake holders.
- Clean, Green and Safe plant &
- Thrilled world society

WORKING STYLE: Pure Indian Ayurveda (2222)

2 hours = plant Visit

2 hours = Meeting/discussion with Team

2 Hours = Thinking for proactive action Plan

2 hours = Assignments delegation & review

MONTHLY PACKAGE:

Slap & Clap with six digit monetary support for family survival.

LOCATION: Anywhere in India

WORKING DAYS: 10 hours x 6 days/week

PROMOTION: In the same field up to Director level

SHORT TERM TARGET: Transform ONE mother Plant

LONG TERM TARGET: Transform all plants & Create 3 more HEAD-AOMS

MANDATE: Minimum 3 years of working in same company/group

HE ASKED ME— "ARE YOU INTERESTED?"

I TOLD—YES, WHY NOT?

WHAT ARE YOUR VIEWS?

18. Inventory Diseases—In SMEs

In the month of Feb'18, I have visited 9 SMEs plants for assessing them to adopt for continual improvement journey. More wishing, less commitments from top management. Some are expecting these mission as parallel management (old system will continue & you help for new system with 3 selected employees).

COMMON PROBLEMS:

Excessive, unwanted, suspected, unaccounted & in mixed shapes—inventory at RM, WIP & FG were common at all 9 plants.

ROOT CAUSES WERE ALSO COMMON: 1) Internal 2) External

1) INTERNAL: No product layout, No operations balancing, No preventive maintenance concept, Depends on few specialized skills, No multi skilling, Multi Locational operations, No 5S on floor & in operations, Moderate grades RM, Poor tool management, manual material handling,,

2) EXTERNAL: No scientifically & Statistically based market projections, Poor vendor performance, Vendors capability to meet their requirements on time, Always choose for lower price supplier only, Poor Material planning.

19. Make Better Decisions for Better Future!

Define goals & Priorities.

Explore ideas & opportunities.

Challenge assumptions.

Investigate realities.

Decide & take actions.

Evaluate your satisfactions!

Spring is on its way and change is coming. Believe it. Don't give up! The sign of real maturity is when you start understanding small things

(Benefits of 5S & Kaizen culture) like facial expression & body language of your employees. Miracles do occur but one has to work hard for them to happen!

20. MANUFACTURING has 4 VEDAS: साम, दाम, दण्ड, भेद!!

Let us consider,

F = Improvement Force = Growth of the Plant

R = Resistance Force = Loss for the Plant

F = R, No change in situation, but difficult to survive,

F < R , Deterioration of the Plant

F > R, Improvement of the Plant

F > R is the only solution for survival and improvement of the plant to remain in the business.

But how to achieve this?

Apply साम, दाम, दण्ड, भेद!!

Employees should be:

Paid well, mentored, challenged, promoted, involved, Appreciated, valued, Empowered, cared, Trusted.

If these tools not work: झटका दें!!

सड़े पान को कतरने में ही भलाई है, नहीं तो सारे पत्ते सड़ जायेंगे!!

21. Not Different, But, Differently!

If you are not THINKING differently, will not survive!

If you are not PLANNING differently, will not survive!

If you are not DESIGNING differently, will not survive!

If you are not TOOLING differently, will not survive!

If you are not MANUFACTURING differently, will not survive!

If you are not TESTING/VALIDATING differently, will not survive!

If you are not CONTROLLING COST differently, will not survive!

If you are not TRAINING differently, will not survive!

If you are not SELLING differently, will not survive!

If you are not ACTING differently, will not survive!!

HERE DIFFERENTLY MEANS MUCH BETTER THAN OTHERS!

IF YOU ARE NOT UNIQUE, YOU WILL NOT SURVIVE, OTHERWISE ALL CVs/BIO-DATA CONTAINING SAME WORD, WHY THEY WILL SELECT YOU??……!!………, He told during interview!!!

22. Objective of Cycle Time Study

Main purpose of cycle time study is for line/operation balancing, not for over production.

Improvement of operation throughput is useless, if the line throughput is not improved. Long hour's machine running for the purpose of utilising idle workforce should not be the objective of line supervisor. Hourly production monitoring of the line is the best, in place of end of the shift or day!

23. Optimisation of Layout

Can reduce manufacturing cost by 6% minimum which will directly boost the PROFITABILITY!

U-shaped layout with single piece flow! Numbers of WIP trolleys reduction is one step of profitability improvement! Poor controls on packing/packaging materials are first sign of loss making company.

Racks for rest, trollies for motion! When we provide racks means we are planning to give good rest to materials and dust & both are big enemy of profitability!

Racks—◆—pallets—◆—trolley—◆—◆conveyor—◆—◆-/ online packing/labelling !

Make reckless company……,,, fat less company !

24. "Profit"–◆–By Yoga!!

It is main mission of any business. Now-a-days, it is important reason of any relationship. It is treated as main source of inspiration. It is prime locomotive for any continual efforts.

The birth of profit:

It comes from selling of products, it comes from robust processing, it comes from good Team, it comes from optimisation of cost, and it comes from elimination of wastes. It comes from economical buying, economically processing and at higher price selling.

How to get in our plant?

Develop a good team under good leadership.

Ensure all processes have robust **SOPs.**

SOPs must be reviewed after any changes.

Controlling point and monitoring points.

Linked these points to every employee's KRA

All cost heads must be optimised and assigned to related departments and leaders.

Wastes identification and elimination team should work continuously for harping excellence.

Innovate and add new features in your products at reduced cost.

Process, product and system audits findings should be treated as main agenda of board meetings.

IT ALL CAN BE POSSIBLE ONLY MAINTENANCE OF EXCELLENT "5S"!

PLEASE BELIEVE "5S" IS THE YOGA OF MANUFACTURING SYSTEM!!

25. (2017-18) Passed... (2018-19) Coming!

ARE WE PREPARED TO FACE THE NEW HEAT, THE NEW TARGET??

HOW?

WILL DRIVE LIKE LAST YEAR? THEN, YOU WILL GET SAME (NOT NEW)!

My learnings (2017–18):

The Past cannot be changed!

Opinions don't define your reality!

Everyone's journey is different!

Things always get better with time!

Judgements are a confession of character!

Over thinking will lead to sadness!

Happiness is found within!

Positive thoughts create positive things!

Smiles are contagious!

Kindness is free!

You will fail, if you quit!

What goes around comes around!

Only dead fish goes with flow, strike your own way!

And my ways would be to support SMEs as a Consultant cum Team leader for their survival & growth!!

26. Value Addition

VALUE ADDITION CFT/MDT

Every plant must have cost/expenses list of repetitive nature expenses.

Pareto analysis is to be done.

Select Top 5 from Top,

Designate experienced, knowledgeable, willing person as team leader for each project (long term basis).

Revise his JD accordingly and help for preparing control point (CP) and Action point (AP).

Delegate this improvement activity with responsibility and authority.

Assure him for financial support with short approval route.

Counter sign his improvements action plan (action point target date & responsibilities with frequent prefixed review frequency).

Set the kick off date.

Meet him every day for few minutes to ask him about any support required for timely completion of identified/selected project.

Arrange for PowerPoint presentation of progress report.

Motivate all team members publicly and highlight the team achievements at prompt location of the plant with photographs.

Introduce him/them to your customers/suppliers.

Celebrate even small achievement!

Let us start from today. Navratri is going on…the best day to start …the best way to start.

27. "World Health Day!"

HEALTH = स्वास्थ्य

Healthy MIND in healthy BODY! Keeping FIT body needs disciplined life style in Diet and exercise.

When body will be unhealthy, mind will be unhealthy. An unhealthy mind takes late and wrong decision. Wrong decision means cost addition. Additional cost is Loss, reduction in PROFIT

Reduced profit is enemy of any business.

So, in a nut shell,

HEALTH = PROFIT

Have we introduced Yoga classes, LAUGHTER THERAPY, 5 minutes morning exercise in our DWM? Before starting of the shift? Are we maintaining BP and sugar level records of all employees on regular basis? Our canteen food quality is being monitored on regular basis as per calories based check point? Our sample size is correct for input checks of foods? Are we providing clean and pure water to our employees? PH value is being monitored and maintained honestly. Who checks finger nails conditions?

If, HEALTH = PROFIT then we must do something concrete for maintaining good health of all employees.

Kindly share some health related best practices in comments!

28. Committed Management – A Boon

Yesterday was my scheduled visit to one plant 60 km away from my house. I started early and reached at committed time. After closing meeting at 5.30 pm, I felt highly satisfied due to following reasons:-

1. MD and Coordinator were present in the factory on time.
2. Last week homework completion ranging from 16 to 80%.
3. Sold 6 trucks (fully loaded) unwanted stocks/materials.
4. Took decision to dispose 4 machines (out of order/old machines).
5. Many metallic trolleys taken out for dismantling and disposal.
6. Six Moulding machines are still in stoppage condition to liquidate excess and unbalanced inventory.
7. Paint procurement stopped for 2 months (except for 1or 2 most wanted but less stock).
8. Pull system started and FG vehicles rotations increased by 4 times.
9. Packing materials, stickers' procurement also stopped for 1 month.
10. Electric wiring localised covers on rotating spindles—works were taken as decided during last visit.
11. Spent 30k on leakages arresting projects.
12. Few metallic almirah, cup-boards rectified to make visible from outside.
13. 22 electric motors also disposed of along with one old motorcycle and 4 metallic gates,
14. Unwanted mounds kept separately for disposal.
15. Shadow board started for tool room.

16. DWM boards introduced as agreed and implementation/use of that board were visible to me.
17. 1S/2S started in office filing too.
18. Deflashing contractor replaced with high efficient and systematic contractor who understands single piece flow mechanism.
19. Productivity improved by 16% in one month without any extra actions except layout change and correct 1S/2S.
20. All team members were very happy at the end of the day and greeted me very happily. They assured me to achieve 100% homework completion on time and every time.

When I was about to leave from there, MD came out from his cabin to see off me in very smiling and happy mood. After 5 minutes of my departure, he sent me "Thank You Sir" one short message.

Yesterday was really great day for me too. I am trying to give 200% to them.

29. Scalar To Vector: A Paradigm Shift Required!

$V = IR$ ————(1)

Voltage increases, Resistance also increases!

Positive force increases, then internal negative force also increases!

$W = F \times D$ ————(2)

Work done = Force x displacement

Looking at both equations, it is very much clear that every plant has some negative people or when you make efforts, there will be always some internal resistance.

One thing is also sure, you cannot eliminate those internal negative forces completely.

Second equation tells, your work can only be recognised when some displacement will happen.

Displacement = some good changes (visually and in balance sheet)

So making positive displacement, only magnitude is not enough but (magnitude + direction) are necessary.

Convert scalar efforts to Vector efforts to get displacement.

I know, you are putting extra efforts/maximum efforts from your side to show the changes in position but it happened?

If yes, then you are in right direction, increase your velocity to reach your target soon.

But, if changes in position not occurred then kindly change the direction of your force, your efforts. You may be pushing near hinge of the door, shift the position, push away from hinge and you will find with less efforts, things have changed.

These directions always come from independent agencies like consultant.

30. Inventory Management: A Real Story of One NCR Company!

1. Sent one month confirmed demand plus 2 months tentative demands to two suppliers (60:40).
2. Instructed delivery schedule on weekly basis (in purchase order)
3. Sent weekly date-wise schedule through mail mentioning max/min quantity permissible entry/day in company, to supplier's executive.
4. Issued precaution letters for way of packaging, acceptable transportation media, mentioning gate entry time/day.
5. Similar instructions passed on to own receipt department and copy to store head.
6. Rack height reduced from 8feet to 3 feet and implemented this for 2 months.
7. Fixed 3 feet racks converted into wheeled trolley and total trolleys counted = 110 no's.

8. After 3 months, no's of trolleys reduced to 35 no's and reduced material handling manpower from 11 to 3.
9. After 6 months total no's of trolleys reduced to 13 no's and attached with small battery operated vehicle with further reduction of manpower from 3 to 2.
10. Roller conveyor length reduced from 7 pcs to 2 pcs parts carrying between two operations
11. After 9 months, conveyor eliminated and put 1 piece flat sheet between two operations

Now they claim

Inventory carrying cost reduced by 82%

Rejection reduced by 88%

Productivity increased by 116%

Profit increased by 22%

They sent: Thank you letter to me!

31. Fit for All – Possible?

Everyone has his own strength and weakness, cannot fit for all purposes. Elephants and horses are not being appreciated by any washer-man, nor are asses invited in marriage ceremony. Yesterday, Mr. Dilpreet, a LinkedIn member, who is following me since last one year, contacted in the evening. "Hello Kumar sir, how are you?"

I am fine, I replied.

Your daily posts are highly useful for many technical persons because you share your own experiences based on different plants visits.

Thanks a lot for your kind appreciation, I again replied.

Are you happy with current assignments? Are you surviving well with consultancy's earnings? he asked very plainly.

I replied back similarly:—I reduced my family expenses to adjust in this situation.

He pointed out promptly, then it's not good. You have immense talent, leadership skill and positive attitude then why don't you think for direct selling concepts like Amway, Vestige and Modi care? You will get very handsome money with fewer efforts. After one year, if you work systematically, you may be reached at Director level, Jaguar clubs, multiple foreign trips

I politely told—brother, I may not fit for that because I don't have such specialised skill sets. I know my SWOT and working on that.

32. Extra Fats in Body or Plants: Both are Dangerous!

Extra fats in body means created house for many diseases like high blood pressure, sugar, high Cholesterol, resulting low life. Doctor always suggests us; keep your body weight exactly as per your height proportion. Lose weight and gain life!

But we never realise that the same system is applicable for our plant life also. Extra fats in plants mean low efficiency, high cost and low profit!

Kindly tell me: what is an objective of business or businessman?

Getting higher profit?

Then how you will achieve that?

Dear friends, kindly reduce fats. These fats are in your inventory, unwanted production, high rejection, obsolete technology, poor work practices, low efficient machines, poor graded materials.

Kindly reduce these fats for survival; otherwise your plants will be no more in coming 3–4 years.

Extra fats always reduce your efficiency and effectiveness. Please think deeply, if as a human you are neither effective nor efficient then what position you will get in your own society? Neglected by all? Right?

The same will happen with your plant. No any new OEM will approach you, even they will not give you date for your plant and process assessment.

I lost 4 kg extra weight, targeting to reduce another 20 kg for my longer life.

33. Consultancy: A New Path for 50+ Years Old Jobless Professionals!

Since Last 3 days, I am suffering from seasonal fever and resting on bed so got enough time to read many value added posts at LinkedIn. Some posts, forced me for introspection like:

1. Dear sir, kindly don't mind, there are 90% Indian LinkedIn members are searching their jobs by writing posts or commenting on others post.
2. Some senior professionals just cutting and pasting articles on DOE, 6-sigma, Taguchi's concept, which are useless for 90% of members.
3. Some seniors opted for providing training and consultancy. Not sure, they like this profession or by they have chosen this for ONLY survival of their family?
4. Few seniors, who have just joined in jobless category, are expressing their frustrations by writing such provoking posts.
5. Every senior are showing that they are masters of World Class mfg system, Quality guru, TPM experts.

What do you think?

I replied: First of all, I am not a master, not an expert, not a Q-guru.

I am not Consultant like any advisor. I adopt that company like extended senior person who owns.

I have chosen as per my interest to mentor many SMEs with my experience.

I am turning to 50, the day I feel, I will join any company at 50% of my last salary, I will do that without any hesitations.

34. 104, Not Out at Stormy Night!

Since last 3 days, I am running at very high fever, excessive body pain and dry coughs. Finally yesterday evening I consulted with my family doctor. Identified reason: moving in heat and different water quality. Took medicines, get sweating and temp came down at 11.30 pm. Now my wife's suggestions started to warn me: What are you doing now? It's 11.30 pm and you are not well. I replied, I am referring dictionary to find out meaning of few words used in this LinkedIn post. She smiled, "so do you think using tough vocabulary is the symbol of highly successful professional? Don't show off, simple and easy communication is the best." She asked me— 3-4 days in a week, you move different part of NCR and frequent temperature changes. Why not you choose one company and work there with full zeal like you do in consultancy? Now you should not ask for designation and comparative package with willing organisation. Health is wealth, if excessive movement is not suitable for you, don't hesitate to rethink and decide new path. I slept after this dose and at 2am again feeling high fever. Key points—choose simple communication method and do PDCA for your decided goal without any hesitation. If you will be healthy, you can serve your family and nation longer. Rethink!

35. Low Cost Automation (LCA)

Low Cost Automation is very string step towards cost optimization journey to improve PQCDSME.

What are different working methods?

MANUAL WORKING = working by man or group = monotonous job = quality & quantity of output *depends upon mood & speed of men* = maximum effectiveness 75% = more cost/unit=chances of more rejection/variable output/hour, low consistency = purely dependant on persons skill.

SEMI AUTO = Partial work by man & partial by machine=better than manual=speed & quality of output slightly better = skill required for setting & output speed depends on machine = quality of output (80% on setting quality & 20% on machine's capability) = moderate mfg cost.

FULLY AUTOMATIC OPERATION = Only loafing & unloading + setting by men, quantity & Quality of output depends on machine capacity & capability = when machine is working, man is not working = watching of machine running is not value addition = lowest mfg cost = quality depends on (80% on capability of machine & 20% on operator's skill for first setting & in process Adjustment when tools wear/breakage) = one man can run many machines at a time. Then which is better to adopt? 1. Judgemental quality, large variety & low volume = Manual is better 2. Better quality, consistent output, lower mfg cost = LOW COST AUTOMATION Choose & use it wisely according to your needs 3. Fully automatic is not always suitable.

36. One More Cost Addition!

To reduce cost, one company has appointed one experienced person but as many other SMEs; this company also has habit for not defining, documenting & implementing the job description of any employees. All are busy without value added works. Spending hours inside the company is the only criteria for getting appreciation in such types of company. I have worked with many SMEs in last two years and 90% are not having culture for job descriptions. They generally appoint so called experienced & specialised skills from similar types of industries. Without JD nobody is responsible for recording, analysis and actions for value addition works. No review, no analysis, everything on experience basis and all wait for MD's instructions.

This coordinator was also doing the same. Many times he reminded me – sir, I come daily at 9 am and leave company at 7 pm.

I just asked: what all activities have you done yesterday? He could not reply confidently because nothing was on black & white. But after hearing his verbal answer I noticed, his 80% times are for moving & talking with different shop in-charges. Walking & chatting are not value addition. Once JD finalised then review of JD effectiveness is also necessary otherwise it will again be one type of another additional cost addition.

37. U – Turn From Improvement Journey!

But I will be on time, let other people come late. "TO DO LIST" is in my mind because I don't carry cooked meal with me. My declared agenda would be: "inconsistent performance & people as liability".

Both are interesting points, agreed? Yes, very burning issues especially in summer season, working at 45 degree on floor. Inconsistent performance is not a new problem but it's consistent. 1or 2 days good production, 1 or 2 days good quality, 1 or 2 days on time delivery. We are very effective for 1or 2 days but not always, why?

Because, it's not in our habit. Consistency can be achieved only through good working environment & culture. Attitude problem too.

For consultancy, a good calibre, dedicated, excited, motivated, target focused, positive thinking, energetic & devoted team required. I am not mentioning here about qualifications & knowledge but attitude, which differentiate from assets & liability. Right people first, no discussion at this point. The right people don't need to be highly managed or fired up. They will be self-motivated with inner drive to produce the best & consistent results. So why I will train there for "DMAIC" first, if RM is not good & known to all. I don't want to prove myself.

38. Dustless SMEs are Profitable!

Dustless means, profitable company. Mostly SMEs are struggling to get good profit because they are not dustless. If you are not dustless then quality complaints are bound to come. Having more complaints resulted low orders, low business shares.

Painting companies are more prone to dust rejections and generally those types are SMEs are in loss.

Source of dusts:

- Soil environment
- More numbers of doors & windows
- All doors & windows are always open
- Shoes from outsides carry additional dusts & muds.
- Grinding operations without localised covers sweeping of floors with brooms, low air pressure inside plants. Packaging boxes also carrying & generating dusts.

How to eliminate it?

Act on surrounding first. Make dustless surrounding by converting soil floor either cemented or green grasses. Ensure closures of all doors & windows, Air curtail to be provided on all entry doors, wet doormats, Doormats cleaning frequently to be increased and cleaned doormats to be ensured outside. To generate positive air pressure inside the plants, doors opening frequency to be drastically reduced. Air washes for visitors. Dust guards for shoes, Wet Mopping in place of broom sweeping. No uncovered grindings to be allowed. Start dust level measurement to monitor the effectiveness of all actions towards it.

39. Forced Deterioration is Unnatural!

Basic reasons of forced deterioration are due to absence of preventive maintenance. Actually, after sometime due to high friction between two surfaces, misalignment of axis, over loading/over capacity utilisation of resources. Generally we are not used to talk with machines/processes so we are unaware with current conditions.

Even in relationship, when we stop communication for some time, friction automatically appears in that.

The basic objective of **TPM** is to increase the life of machines, decrease the rate of wear & tear due to normal deterioration and eliminate the possibility of forced deterioration.

During analysis of minor stoppage, we come across reasons like jam, over heated, one sided excessive wear & tear, loosening, noisy. By real implementation of **JISHU HOZEN** (step 1, 2 & 3) all forced deterioration related FUGUAI can be arrested and by implementation of periodic maintenance & preventive maintenance, it can be shifted to normal deterioration categories.

Pre-matured failure is the real culprit for lower OEE/OLE. *Cleaning of outer body of machines or panel will not help for downtime reduction.*

"CLITA" is just like machine yoga. Cleaned without cleaning, Ganga flow, Auto lubrication, trained eyes for fuguai detection & corrections.

40. Zero "BAD" is the Goal for "TPM"!

B = Breakdown

A = Accident

D = Defect

Zero is the target for getting this award. TPM is not a certificate but an award for our sustenance efforts. Certificate, in my mind has lost its dignity & respect due to multiple reasons. *Certificate = Qualification ticket*

& as we know, ticket can be purchased by paying charges/fees/cost. Award is totally different thing. Award can be got only by consistent efforts, not by money. Award is the reward for consistent, effective & efficient efforts made by individual or team.

Hitting the goal, one time, may be due to sheer luck too, but consistently achieving the goal is the habit & culture.

TPM is the habit, a culture for maintaining effective & efficient results. We should not try to purchase this. Efforts can't be purchased but only can be gained.

ZERO is the unique number, it's positioning is very crucial. If we keep at left, the situation is same as earlier but when we place it at right for right mission, the value increases exponentially.

Talking **ZERO** is very easy but achieving & maintaining **ZERO** is very hilly task. It can be achieved only through dedicated & committed discipline, not only by knowledge or skill only. It will come only from practice, so TPM is the name of rigorous practice.

BAD is an extra COST.

41. TPM: Another certification like ISO-9001?

Recalling the period of early 90s, when ISO was really hallmark for QMS implementations and companies were treated as pioneer in their fields. In late 90s, TPM started to register their presence in India under guidance of JIPM-TPM guru Sueo Yanaguchi san.

8 pillars were taught and implemented through cluster approach. I was representing on behalf of one North Indian Clutch manufacturing company.

JISHU HOZEN (Autonomous Maintenance) was the first & the most important pillar for restoring & maintaining the machine's basic (as new) conditions. DIS-COVER to DISCOVER was the first lesson.

Red tagging was the methodology. CLITA was the objective of JISHU HOZEN.

"C" of CLITA stands for Cleaning, having very deeper meaning with these questions: why to clean? What to clean, where to clean, who will clean, when it should be cleaned & finally how to clean? These clarification and implementation were very eye opener example. New machines look like new, what is surprising in this? Motto of JH was, if old machines look like new and performing like new or not? Learnt the real engagement of TEI (Total Employees Involvement) or TEE (Total Employees Engagement). After all red tags removal by team, we visualise that now machine is looking like fresh new machine with high efficiency and zero B/D.

42. दो जून की रोटी: सविता भाभी

सविता भाभी is the symbol of today's home maker lady of any houses of common families of India whose husbands, brothers or sons are struggling to get a job for their family survival. They are so called "educated, experienced, honest, dedicated and hardworking" candidates whose futures are not sure even to provide "दो जून की रोटी" to their families.

We, INDIAN, are unique by natures. We are confused, we are good followers. We are not innovators; even we are not good implementers. We are confused between process and results.

RPN of FMEA is to be implemented on "दो जून की रोटी" also. RPN of suitable job finding & sustenance was never 1(one) but now it is touching to 1000 for many. Who will get the interview call, who will get the job even who will sustain in any jobs, all are in dilemma. No one is sure; all are scared, resulted job cutting in the name of cost savings. Very few Management are working towards manufacturing more & selling more. Mostly are working on only saving more. In this race, they make mistakes in deciding "COSTS Vs VALUES".

Cost reduction has limit to zero but value addition has no upper limits.

In 50 years, we have not implemented real "5S" on floor, our national agenda are still

"स्वच्छ भारत,स्वस्थ भारत !
जागो भारत, जागो !
पीढ़ी को बचाओ!!

43. Knowledge: Attitude: Courage!

Simplicity is the *best*, Complicated is the *waste*. Visionary means not always talking about imaginary thing but proactively thinking for outcome & their remedial actions at planning stage. Learning from past and implementing those experiences in planning.

I met many failed knowledgeable person in my professional career. They know everything well regarding different manufacturing systems, tools & techniques but never succeed to translate that knowledge on floor. Their knowledge never accepted & respected. Never contributed in team building and corporate goal achievements, why?

Because when I look back his style, he was complex man. He used to prepare complex formats for recording & monitoring. He was shy to analyse data through histogram, bar chart, scatter diagram, stratification but always talking about DMAIC, DFM, and DOE, without considering the team understanding capability.

Less skill & less knowledge are not the serious problem but not understanding our audience is the biggest problem. Low cost automation is also a good solution for productivity & quality improvement in place of robotisation of simple mfg process. Cycle time reduction without thinking for line balancing is the sheer waste of time & money. Be courageous to implement your simple thought.

44. Total Experience Management (TEM)!

Experience is an investment, not always cost. Total experience is the combinations of:

1. Failure & winning stories,
2. Love & hate stories
3. Accepted, respected & neglected stories
4. Chasing, purchasing & selling stories
5. Thinking, designing, creating & destroying stories
6. Meeting, sitting, deciding, accepting & avoiding stories,
7. Winning & losing stories

In all such cases, there are some gains & pains, some costs & investments, some sharing & shedding.

Getting new job or circumstances of quitting old jobs are another type of experience.

TEM is an art, not a science. Failing makes deeper impacts on our life and anyone can learn from their failure stories, if they are capable to identify the real root cause.

Not getting a job, even carrying in-depth knowledge, required skills, supported with rich experience, then what could be the real reasons?

This question is really a genuine but have we answered?

No, because such question requires advanced problem solving techniques, like Six sigma, Affinity diagram, Fault tree analysis.

Kindly tell me truthfully, have you seen such analysis with countermeasures (like case studies at LinkedIn?)-No

Identify the real root cause & take mistake proofing countermeasure is the real essence of " TEM"!

45. Voltage = Current × Resistance

$$V = IR$$

Voltage is directly proportional to current

Voltage = Inputs = Man, Machine, Material, Money, Method, Measurement system & Working environment

Current = Output = Products, Services

Resistance = Hurdles = Negative minded people, Lower skill level, internal politics, the breakdown of machines, poor quality of raw materials, bad working environment, etc

Kindly think about the above-mentioned equation.

Suppose,

V = 449 volt

R = 0 ohm

The Current will be zero.

Resistance is regarded as constant. When you will increase voltage, resistance will also increase.

So, resistance can be only minimized but can't be eliminated.

In other words, if there is zero resistance then no voltage (positive force) required.

Voltage in management terms means excellent 6 M + Excellent Environment

How to reduce resistance?

Appoint positive mind, establish positive & motivated working environment, no compromises with discipline, validated SOP for all processes, responsibility + accountability + authority at all levels, Training, assessment, recognition, celebration, penalty for bad performance, career opportunity, growth roadmap, Reward for honesty, Poka-yoke in systems through continual audits & reviews.

Transparent & unbiased communication.

Positive acts!

46. Thinking Lean: Talking Lean: Doing Lean: Practicing Lean!

Nobody can claim that he is a master at it. No 2nd Toyota so far in last 50 years, why?

Answers are very simple: our thinking, talking, doing & practicing are different for different customers, for different employees, for different shifts.

We are not honest to any system: process, people & products!

We know everything except we don't know what we should know. We are addicted to showing nature. You can check it, go to the Engineering department & ask them:—❖—

- Do you know correctly, what is 5S?—yes
- Do you know? SPC, MSA, FMEA, APQP, PPAP, and Calibration— yes?
- Do you know? TQM, LEAN manufacturing, TQM, TQC, TCM, TOC—yes!
- Have you documented & approved? QMS, Policy, control plan, checkpoint, work instructions, OPL, SOP—yes!
- Management is willing to implement all these?—yes!
- You are interested to implement these on the floor?—yes!
- Have you started anything?—yes!

Show me!

He pointed out slogans on the wall: Customer is the king, we are process focused, Safety first, First-time right Quality, and motivated employees are assets…

And at the same place: suspected materials, loose wiring, leakages below the machine, overloaded material trolley, no localized lighting for visual inspection, batch production, zig-zag layout, uncalibrated instruments.

47. Use or Remove

In reading, these words (Use or remove) are very simple & common but the impact of implementation is very tough & time taking.

Generally, people fail to decide on these two simple words and continue as earlier.

Burnt electric motors, fused tube lights, broken window glass, High energy consuming machines, negative mind people, low efficient supervisor, suspected machines spare parts, red/grey materials inventory, expired shelf life paints, chemicals………….!

Why it takes time?

Keeping for a long time is cost addition or value addition?

We all know, it is a cost addition!

Still not decided, what is the real problem?

Don't we have time for a decision?

We all know, we have excess time for non-value added activities.

Are we not getting right scrap dealer on time?

There are many in our locality & can come on a simple phone call or single sentence mail!

Then, why still not decided and implemented?

Lack of interest?

You have many more important works apart from these?

What are those more important works than this?

These are profit eaters, time eaters, and morale eaters but

Still, we want to continue like this?

It means, we have decided to sink our profitability, decided to make dirty, dangerous, difficult, and demotivated & loser plants?

ON TIME & RIGHT DECISION are KEYS for PROFIT

48. Spc Management

SPC = Stable, Predictable & Capable!

Processes having all these characters are an ideal process. Great processes have capability indices more than 1.67.

Stability is the first criteria to assess the capability of a process. Predictability is the inbuilt criteria, Stable processes can be good or bad, having **"common causes,"** which are permanent in natures, having many small sources of variations and shall be permanent until actions taken.

Special causes have one or a few sources of variations, maybe irregular & unpredictable in nature, may appear unless actions are taken.

All Stable and predictable processes may not be capable. It has an irregular shape, wider spread & shifted locations.

R-chart: Any point beyond a control limit is the signal for immediate analysis of the operation for the special cause. Mark any data points that are beyond control limits for further investigation and corrective actions.

A point above the upper control limit for ranges is generally a sign that: The control limit has been miscalculated or wrongly plotted, piece to piece variability or the measurement system has changed (a different inspector or gauge).

A point below the lower limit: May be due to wrong plotting, spread changed or measurement system changed.

49. Types of Management!

- Making less + selling more = **Adjusting Management**
- Making less + selling less = **Deteriorative Management**
- Making more + selling more = **Progressive Management**
- Making more + selling more + Thinking more = **Optimistic Management**
- Making more+ selling more + Thinking mire * Innovating more = **Visionary management**
- Making more + selling more + Thinking more + innovating more + Planning more = **Missionary management**
- Making more + Selling more + Thinking more + Innovating more + planning more + Organising more = **Creative Management**
- Making more+ selling more + Thinking more + Innovating more + planning more + Organising more + Delegating more = **Authentic Management**
- Making more + selling more + Thinking more + Innovating more + Planning more + Organising more + Delegating more + Reviewing more = **Superlative Management**
- Making more + selling more + Thinking more + Innovating more + Planning more + Organising more + Delegating more + Reviewing more + Motivating more = **Ideal Management** + celebrating more = **Imaginary management**!!

Are you an imaginary Management, no?

Want to become? Try it!!

SELECT 10 PROJECTS FROM THIS BOOK TO IMPLEMENT IN YOUR PLANT THAT IS THE REAL GOAL OF MY BOOK WRITING!!

My best wishes,

With Love,

S.B. KUMAR
Author of: FIX 'n' FINISH
PRE-FIT for PROFIT

www.ingramcontent.com/pod-product-compliance
Lightning Source LLC
Chambersburg PA
CBHW020909180526
45163CB00007B/2685